Sabine Baring-Gould

The Queen of Love

Vol. I

Sabine Baring-Gould

The Queen of Love
Vol. I

ISBN/EAN: 9783337040932

Printed in Europe, USA, Canada, Australia, Japan

Cover: Foto ©ninafisch / pixelio.de

More available books at **www.hansebooks.com**

THE QUEEN OF LOVE

THE QUEEN OF LOVE

A NOVEL

BY

S. BARING-GOULD

AUTHOR OF
'MEHALAH,' 'IN THE ROAR OF THE SEA,'
ETC., ETC.

IN THREE VOLS.

VOL. I.

Methuen & Co.
36 ESSEX STREET, W.C.
LONDON
1894

CONTENTS

CHAP.		PAGE
I.—The Deputation,		1
II.—How the Deputation fared,		11
III.—Old Hall Field,		23
IV.—Rab Rainbow,		37
V.—"Hammer" Grice,		46
VI.—The Circus,		58
VII.—Rab to the Rescue,		70
VIII.—Nuts,		79
IX.—Brother or no Brother?		92
X.—An Orphan,		105
XI.—Ada Button,		116
XII.—Rab's Right,		126
XIII.—No! No! No!		135
XIV.—Beggar-My-Neighbour,		145
XV.—Again: Beggar-My-Neighbour,		155
XVI.—The Tight-Rope,		165

THE QUEEN OF LOVE

THE QUEEN OF LOVE

―――o―――

CHAPTER I.

THE DEPUTATION.

A SINGLE cab or fly—that was the sole equipage let out on hire in the town of Saltwich.

It had an arrangement whereby it could appear with a pair on very solemn occasions. Usually it wore shafts, between which shuffled one horse.

The fly was painted black, and when engaged for a funeral it had a cushion and vallance of black for the box. The interior was lined with a very deep green, so deep that when the black trimmings were on the box it might be thought that the whole vehicle was plunged in the inkiest depths of woe.

But when the fly was required for a wedding, then the cushions and vallance on the box were of a cheerful green, and the interior drapery brightened up into a corresponding smile.

But the fly was also engaged, occasionally, by such persons as did not keep carriages, to convey them to country houses to make calls. On such occasions the driver assumed a hat with a broad gold band, and a greatcoat with armorial brass buttons; moreover, the proprietor applied to the side a red lion passant, surmounted by a coronet. On being called out for a funeral, the driver wore a hat muffled in crape. When he conducted a wedding-party, he wore a favour of white ribbons. At elections he wore sometimes an orange and blue, sometimes a red rosette, according as he was engaged, along with his cab, by the Liberal or the Conservative parties.

The driver was out at the precise moment and day and year on which this story opens, lightly touching up his one horse between the shafts, and he wore no distinguishing badge of mirth or woe. The cab contained three men in their best suits—the suits in which they attended chapel on Sundays, and appeared on platforms at temperance or missionary meetings.

The driver, whose face was flexible as gutta-percha, had accommodated his features to his fare. He looked as serious as though engaged in the undertaking business. His nose was pointed along the axis of the spine of his horse; nevertheless, his eyes turned into the corners to observe an immense illustrated poster representing the achievements of horses, dogs and men belonging to a travelling circus.

"Stop! Stop!"

A head emerged from the right side of the cab. The head was that of a man of nearly sixty. He had very dark hair growing thickly over his head and neck, and below his chin. He was closely-shaved on the jaws and about the mouth. His eyes were dark, his face square, his features heavy.

"Stop! Stop!"

A head emerged from the left side of the cab. The head was covered with sandy hair, the eyes were of a watery blue, the cheek florid. The man was stout, and had a short neck.

The obedient driver drew up.

Both heads were drawn in.

Then the dark-haired man addressed a man with the face of a sheep, who sat with his back to the horses.

"Mr Poles, will you get out, and with your umbrella scrape down that abominable placard? It is indecent!"

"Do, please, Mr Poles. It will serve as a protest," said the sandy-haired man.

"Must I?" asked the gentleman with the sheep's head.

"Indeed, indeed you must. We will wait for you. Thomas shall not drive on. Consider the privilege,

Poles, of putting away evil. Act up to your name. Be a Phineas; use your umbrella."

Thus adjured, the sheep-faced man stumbled out over the knees of the dark occupant of the back seat, and proceeded to efface the placard with the ferrule of his umbrella.

"It's rather large," said he, "and the paste is adhesive."

"Rip it down," advised the fair-haired man.

"Jump and lay hold of the shreds, and you will peel off large pieces," urged the dark man.

Some boys began to collect and utter protests. A handful of mud thrown by one urchin, who had secreted himself behind the carriage, struck Mr Poles in the small of the back.

"Poles!" called one of the inmates of the cab, "you had better return to us. The Moabites are upon us. We will drive on."

Accordingly, the sheep-faced witness to decorum re-entered the cab.

"Go on, Thomas," said the dark head at one window.

"You may drive on," said the sandy head at the other window.

Meanwhile, a labouring man, standing near the front wheel of the vehicle, asked the driver whom he was conveying.

"It's a deputation," answered the coachman, without turning his head.

THE DEPUTATION

"And what monkey-tricks be this bloomin' deputation after?" further inquired the workman.

"It's goin' to protest agin' the circus, and stop it, if it can, from comin' into Saltwich."

"Thomas! I said 'drive on!'" called the dark-haired, interior passenger from the left window.

"Do you hear? Drive on!" said the fair-haired passenger from the right window.

The labouring man, looking steadily at the face on the left, said,—

"Oh! that's Jabez Grice." Then he caught sight of the sandy-haired man on the right, and said, "So! Nottershaw is one of this deputation. And Poles," he added, as his eye caught the side-face of the sheep-like man with his back to the horses.

The driver had described his fare concisely and accurately. He was, in fact, conveying a deputation commissioned by the Seriously-Minded of the town of Saltwich, and that deputation consisted of the quintessence of that body—the cream, the core of all that was respectable and sedate. Out of rude, common life, the ore was laboriously extracted by the efforts of the various ministers of the several denominations in Saltwich. The fine gold of perfect humanity thus obtained was run into the moulds of the different denominational chapels. But just as an alchemist who sublimates gold draws from it one essential, nay, super-essential drop, so did each congregation of the

Seriously-Minded, on distillation, yield up a quintessence; and such drops of superlative excellence were the three gentlemen who formed the deputation—Mr Jabez Grice, foreman of Messrs Brundrith's Salt Works; Mr John Nottershaw, architect, builder, contractor and surveyor; and Mr Phineas Poles the paperhanger.

Saltwich was a Cheshire Jerusalem, whither the tribes of the Seriously-Minded went up to deepen their gravity, build up their self-assurance, and sharpen the severity with which they judged their neighbours.

Unhappily there were tares among the wheat, dross along with the gold—a certain number in the place who could not be purged of their grossness, however vigorously the bellows might be blown and the rakes applied. Resolutely and defiantly they maintained their levity.

If it had been possible to have accommodated all the Seriously-Minded along one side of the street, and relegated the frivolous to the other side, it would have been satisfactory. But practically this was not feasible. A veritable puss-in-the-corner, or prisoners' bass, was played in Saltwich. Some of the most worldly became for a while grave, and passed over to the side of the sedate; then some of the seriously-disposed relapsed, and were found in the congregation of the frivolous. It was not possible, geographically, to circumscribe or distribute the two classes. And yet, to a limited extent, such a separation had been effected, and one portion of Saltwich went vulgarly by the name of Jewry, another by that of Heathendom. The eminently serious had succeeded in securing most of the offices of authority and trust in the place, and they had established an outward semblance of gravity in the town. The only large hall in Saltwich was under their control, and no theatrical performances, no nigger-minstrelsy, no public dances were ever suffered to take place within its walls. Nothing was tolerated beneath its roof more sportive than a missionary meeting, more entertaining than dissolving views of Palestine.

A quiver of dismay ran through austere Saltwich when it was blazed abroad on every hoarding, and at every street-corner, that the circus of Signor Giuseppi Santi, with galloping ostriches, naked Indians, performing dogs, short-skirted dancers, clowns, trapezists, bounders through fiery hoops, was about to enter the town, erect its booths, and give a performance—and that, moreover, on the very evening upon which the renowned Rev. Dr Tallow of Jericho, U.S.A., was advertised to give an impressive undenominational and awakening exercise in the Town Hall, with the approval of all denominations in Saltwich.

It was such a privilege to have, for one night, Dr Tallow in their midst. It was so important to give him an united, an enthusiastic reception. It was so advisable to impress on the reverend doctor the intense seriousness of the inhabitants—and now, on that very day when the Rev. Dr Tallow entered the town at one side, slightly-draped damsels and men in fleshings, clowns in paint and powder, and piebald ponies would be entering it on the other side; and, what was worst of all, at the very time that the Rev. Dr Tallow was to coruscate in his most brilliant periods, pirouette at the apex of his loftiest elocution—at that very time, within a stone's cast of the hall, a circus with painted Jezebels and half-draped Bathshebas, and every description of allurement that the wicked world could offer, would be attracting to it the young and the thoughtless.

The sting of the consideration lay in the fact just alluded to, that the circus would be planted within a stone's throw of the Town Hall.

Owing to the frequent and protracted subsidences of the land as the salt rock beneath the town was extracted, the Old Town Hall had gone to pieces, and had sunk half-way up its first floor, and had to be pulled down. Then a New Town Hall had been erected on higher ground, on a space that was considered secure. As there was open ground hard by, the proprietor of the circus had obtained permission from the proprietor of the field to erect his booth thereon, and there display his attractions. It must be allowed that he had made his arrangements in complete ignorance of the fact that the Rev. Dr Tallow was to hold forth in the Town Hall that same evening.

The elect did not feel anxious for themselves. They feared for the wavering. They feared for the young. They feared for the nibblers. They feared for their own sons and daughters, for their domestics and shop-boys.

The Seriously-Minded put their heads together. What was to be done? To postpone the visit of the eminent American preacher would be an acknowledgment of defeat. To run Dr Tallow against Signora Muslina was risky. To the Seriously-Minded, of course, no hankering after the circus could occur. They would all be found on the benches or on the platform—but how about their young people? Would not they take advantage of the absence of their elders to rush to the circus?

Again, owing to the proximity of the circus, was it not likely that the strains of Signor Santi's brass band playing the "Rogues' March" might be heard within the hall, and overpower the sighs and groans of the listeners to the reverend doctor? that "Pop goes the Weasel" might disturb the effect produced by his most impressive applications? that the cheers and hand-clapping at some dexterous feat of a trapezist or hoop-jumper might distract the attention of the auditors and set them, in their minds, lusting after the vanities of the circus?

Accordingly, the various denominations squeezed themselves to produce their finest elixir, and this fine elixir was deputed to see Mr Button, the farmer owning his own land, to whom belonged the plot whereon the circus was to be erected, and to induce him to withdraw it from the equestrian troupe.

CHAPTER II.

HOW THE DEPUTATION FARED.

MR BUTTON was apparently a well-to-do man. He had set up brick gate-posts in alternating bands of white and red, and elaborate cast-iron gates at the entrance to his drive, and had planted his drive with shrubs, which, however, did not thrive vigorously, owing to the fumes from the chimneys of the Salt Works. He had rebuilt his house. It was as square in base as the pyramid of Ghizeh but not so secure, for the whole district of the Weaver Valley rested on beds of salt rock, and as that salt rock was corroded by water, and then sucked out in the form of brine by the steam pumps, the surface of the country sank correspondingly. Mr Button, prepared for this contingency, had built his house in the Cheshire fashion, with timber and brick. His foundations consisted of stout oak beams laid on the soil, extending somewhat beyond the lines of his walls. The advantages of this method of construction lay in the fact that, should a subsidence take place, his house would not split and fall about his head, but would lurch and settle either sideways or backwards or forwards, bodily, and then it would be possible to escape from it without danger.

The salt rock of the Cheshire beds is sixty-three feet thick; the height of Saltwich about forty feet above the sea; consequently the withdrawal of sixty-three feet of rock threatened, in time, to send that tract of country under sea level.

Consider yourself in bed and snug on a mattress with a palliasse below, and that some practical joker were to draw the palliasse from under you; you would sink the full thickness of the withdrawn bed of straw. So, in the Cheshire district, the inhabitants rest above a mattress of marl, lying over a palliasse of salt rock. The manufacturers draw out from under them this bed of rock, and down settle the inhabitants many feet deeper than they were before. Sometimes they descend slowly, sometimes they go down with a jerk.

The way in which this letting down of the surface of the land is performed is ingenious, and those whose properties are affected can obtain no redress. It is not brought about by mining—that is to say, no mining done by pick and shovel. What is done is to sink a shaft to where the brine overlies the rock, and pump it up. As this goes on night and day, so night and day the water is washing more of the rock till, the whole being dissolved, the whole has been removed in a solution and sent away in the form of salt. In time Mr Button must expect his entire estate to be submerged; but it would probably last his time. He must have a house to cover him, so he had rebuilt his dwelling-house in such manner as to let him down easily when it did sink. Meanwhile, Mr Button did what he could with his land, and did not do badly. He had a large dairy; he made butter, and would have made cheese, had not the consumption of milk and butter in Saltwich been so great that he could do more profitably by selling the raw and partially-manufactured produce of the cow, than by converting it into cheese. And though his land might be going down under his feet, as far as could be judged, his means were rising. He owned a parcel of land, as already said, close to the New Town Hall. Indeed, the site for this New Town Hall had been purchased of him.

The deputation drove in at Mr Button's entrance. The coachman had descended from the box and had rolled back the new iron gates; but somehow the catch did not answer, the fact being that the ground had given way since this catch had been set, so that the man was constrained to hold open the valve and call to his horse to proceed.

The horse dutifully walked forward.

"Way!" called the driver.

The horse did not hear the call, or mistook it, for it quickened its pace and began to trot along the drive.

"Halloo! you darned crocodile!" yelled the coachman, letting go the gate, and running after the cab. Then, considering this objurgation out of keeping with his appearance and the character of his fare, he called "Stay, my dearly-beloved brother!"

The horse, offended at the first epithet, and not mollified by the second address, trotted still faster. It did not halt at the door of the house, but trotted on past it, past the shrubs, out into a field, with the deputation behind it, flinging itself about through the windows, grappling at the door handles, shouting remonstrances to the horse in front, and cries to the driver running behind, and was suddenly arrested by a hand on the bit. The arrest was so sudden that Mr Poles was precipitated against the two other members of the deputation.

"Now, then," exclaimed Mr Button, coming to the door of the cab, "what are you gents after? Have you taken tickets for the bottomless pit, and are in a desperate haste to be at your destination?"

"Oh, sir, will you drag out Mr Poles? Take him piecemeal if you will. He is smothering us!"

Mr John Nottershaw butted at the paperhanger with his head, and managed by brute force to drive him back-foremost out at the door, and then he emerged himself in a somewhat rumpled condition.

"The horse ran away," he explained.

"The horse was curious, no doubt, to see what has happened. Justifiable under the circumstances."

"What has happened?" asked Mr Nottershaw.

"Come and see for yourselves. What! is that Jabez Grice? Halloo! What brings you here? Let me see—one, two, three of you all in your Sunday-go-to-meeting togs, and coming in the cab also! What's in the wind? Money? Subscriptions? I've none. I've lost one of my finest Jerseys. Come and see. I had her brought from the Channel Islands; she cost me a large sum, and now—I can't even get her hide for tanning, or horns and hoofs for gelatine. But, bless me! what have you driven in the cab for?"

Mr Button might well ask; the distance from Saltwich was inconsiderable. The fact was that the deputation had engaged the vehicle so as to give weight to their representations.

"We have not come for money," said Mr Grice with dignity. "We have come as representatives of a large portion of the inhabitants of Saltwich to lay before you our views."

"Let me lay mine before you first, man," said the farmer.

"We have a serious cause of complaint."

"So have I; I've lost my cow. Come along and

look at my grievance. You are in the Salt Works, Jabez, and so are to blame, and should indemnify me. But I know better than to look for indemnification to you salt men. Brundrith says, 'Prove that I did it and I will pay.' But I can't prove that it was Brundrith, and not Hewlett or Elson. I go to Hewlett; he says, 'Show that I did it, I'm a mile and a half from your place; try Elson.' Elson says, 'Convince me it was I—not Brundrith. I am two miles and a half off. We all pump.' There is no redress to be got. I must bite my nails and bear it."

Several men were in the field standing about a conical gap in the surface, at the bottom of which water or mud was in a condition that looked like ebullition, though in reality it was cold.

"Don't go too near," said Button; "the surface is moving, cracking, and more will settle shortly."

"But where is the cow."

"There!" answered the farmer, pointing to the cauldron. "All at once the land gave way whilst my Jersey was cropping the grass, and in the wink of an eye she had disappeared. Where is my cow? You see a hole in the surface where my Jersey was, and she is going down, goodness knows where to, somewhere below there in the bowels of the earth; somewhere, where salt rock was, there is now my Jersey worth forty pounds. That is what comes of your pumping Grice."

"Well, sir! It's a great loss—but you must reckon

HOW THE DEPUTATION FARED

that the salt works bring a market to your door. If you lose in one way, you win in another."

"I know that; I am sick of this concern," cried Button. "If anyone would pay me twelve thousand pounds, he should have the whole bag of tricks. I'll tell you what he ought to do—set up a salt work of his own. Why should Brundrith, Elson and Hewlett suck out all the rock from under our feet? Let us suck against them and make what we can out of our own salt, and that underlying our neighbours. 'Make hay while the sun shines' is the saying. Here we have it—'Get out the salt whilst you can, and the devil take posterity!'"

"You had best do that yourself, Mr Button."

"Not I; I have not the energy nor the experience. Come, Jabez, if you can find the money, you shall have the place, and run against Brundrith and Elson, and make your fortune."

"I have not the money."

"Well, mention my offer to those who have. If I were a younger man, I'd suck at one end and Brundrith at the other, and see which could suck the other down, and suck the wealth to himself."

"Now," said Jabez Grice, "will you listen to what we have to say?"

"By all means; but come from here—we can do no more than lament over my vanished cow and the field which is going after the cow, and will soon be con-

VOL. I. B

verted into a flash.* Come along, into the house, and I will listen to what you have to say."

He led the way to his square residence, the roof of which rose to a point with a block of central chimneys in the midst. The advantage of this arrangement was that the chimneys were propped up on every side. The cabman with his conveyance followed.

As soon as the party was in the nearly square sitting-room, the deputation opened the subject on which it was commissioned to wait on him.

"Oh! about this affair of the circus—I don't see how I'm to get out of it. I've promised the field."

Mr Nottershaw looked at Mr Grice, and the paperhanger looked at first one, and then the other.

"I suppose the agreement is hardly committed to writing?" said Jabez.

"No—but a man's word should be as good as his bond."

"Well—yes—in ordinary circumstances. But there are occasions when no man is bound. No man is bound to commit a sin."

"I don't know how, without disgrace, I can get out of a promise."

Mr Grice rubbed his polished chin.

"It depends on the wording," he said. "I suppose you promised the field by the Town Hall."

* A flash is the local term for a sheet of water where once was dry ground.

"Certainly."

"Did you specify which Town Hall?"

"There is but one. The other has been pulled down."

"That is true, but the situation still bears the name of Town Hall Field."

"The flash is there and the ground is full of cracks."

"I'll tell you what, Button," broke in Nottershaw, "you never did a worse job in your life than encouraging these mountebanks. There are two members of the Weaver Trust will be on the platform of the Rev. Dr Tallow, and they won't thank you; they won't propose you for a trustee at the next vacancy, you may be certain, and that won't be far off—old Whitley is on his last legs. I've heard from a bird who whispers in my ear that you have a fancy to be on the Trust—rather."

"And then," said Mr Grice, "many of the Serious-Minded get their milk and butter—"

"And eggs," threw in Mr Poles.

"Milk, butter and eggs from you; and it would be a pity—a great pity—to offend them. I don't say it would, but it might, affect your pecuniary interests —there is no knowing; it would be unreasonable, still there is no knowing; they might transfer their custom to Ruggles, get him to supply them with butter and milk."

"And eggs," added the paperhanger.

"Butter and milk and eggs," said Grice, again accepting the addition.

"You see, Button," said the builder, "I'm a man of business myself, and I know that it don't do to offend parties which hang together like bees. Honey-bearing they may be, yet sting they can. You'll excuse me, I'm a practical man."

"But what can I do?"

"The matter is clear as rock salt," said Jabez in a peremptory tone. "The Old Town Field is good enough for those ragamuffins. They shall have that or none. A parcel of tight-rope dancers have no right to pick and choose, to say, 'We will have this site, to the disturbance and annoyance of the Seriously-Minded, and we will not have that, which will incommode nobody worth consideration.' Send them where they will be no nuisance."

"But," said the farmer with hesitation, "the old field is not safe. It is at the edge of the flash, and the ground is full of cracks, and is slipping in."

"So much the better—it may deter many from attendance."

"I don't know what to say," said Button, rubbing his head and looking with keen eyes at Jabez Grice. "You see—it was an understanding."

"A misunderstanding, you must let them comprehend. They shall have the Old Hall Field. Nonsense!

Mr Button, you are not so foolish as to trifle away your interests for the sake of a set of mountebanks; they shall go beside the flash, and it will do for them; there will be water there for their horses."

"It is dangerous."

"No harm will come to them—they are there for one night only. Look here, Mr Button, you want to sell your scrap of land. I'll speak to Brundrith, he lays great stress on my opinion. I'll advise him to buy, so as to avoid the chance of competition."

"As you will, gentlemen," said Button. "Let me see, I'll go off to Chester. You must manage for me."

Still his twinkling eye was on Grice.

As the deputation prepared to leave, he crooked in his finger and winked at Jabez. He put his finger through his button-hole and held him back. When the other two were out of hearing, he said,—

"I know there is something behind—do you think I'm a fool? I remember poor Joe Sant—I know him in spite of his Signor, his Giuseppe, his Santi, and all that sort of thing. I suppose, Grice, you don't like that he, your half-brother—"

"He is not even my quarter-brother."

"As you will—your reputed brother should appear in tights and spangles when you are haranguing. Well, it would be a scandal. I'll go away, and you shall block every entrance to my field. Settle with them that they are to rig up their show in Old Hall Field instead of New Hall Field, beside the flash instead of near your meeting. And—mind—remember what you said about Brundrith. I'm sick of living on a sinking soil."

CHAPTER III.

OLD HALL FIELD.

THE loss of the field near the New Town Hall did not greatly affect the spirits of the equestrian troupe, for it did not seem likely to materially affect their prospects. They were of a sanguine disposition, ready to make the best of very adverse circumstances, and the obligation to transfer the scene of their performances from one part of the town to another did not strike them as matter for concern. They were provided with an open space on which to pitch their tents, and this open space was nearer to the densest-populated part of Saltwich than was the site first agreed upon.

Where they now were was on the fringe of the ragged land near the old portion of the town—old, that is to say, comparatively, for the brine springs of Saltwich had not been discovered before the end of the eighteenth century, and the town had sprung up where had once been green fields. The most ancient buildings were comparatively modern and eminently ugly. They consisted of rows of brick cottages, and it was precisely these rows which went locally by the name of Heathendom.

These rows were regarded by the denominations of the grave, who held Saltwich in their grip, as all but hopeless as a hunting-ground. Its inhabitants were wholly given over to insolent, inconsiderate gaiety. Their levity of conduct was a continual offence to the Seriously-Minded. The noise of Heathendom contrasted with the quietude of Jewry. The two moral hemispheres of Saltwich were in perpetual feud. Not a window in Heathendom contained a notice that the great American preacher was about to hold forth in the New Town Hall, and not a blank wall in Jewry displayed the attractions of the horsemanship.

In Heathendom congregated the poachers who ravaged Delamere Forest and provided the hares and rabbits and partridges for the local poulterers, to whom the Seriously-Minded gave their custom, without inquiring too closely whence all this game came.

Two streets had gone to rack and ruin, rifts had formed in the house-walls, and stacks of chimneys had fallen. The grave regarded this as a judgment on the gay who had inhabited them—whilst themselves pumping and steaming and sending away and converting into gold the salt rock that underlay these habitations. If the poor were turned out of their houses, or if they were forced to spend half their time in their bedrooms because their sinking kitchens were flooded—what did it represent to the imaginations of the serious of every denomination, who were themselves securely and dryly housed, but a call addressed by Nature herself to the frivolous to mend their ways.

In Heathendom were crushed and crowded together all such as had been driven out of the condemned and demolished houses; no room was given them in the new and spacious parts of the town, where the houses were of white brick and the windows of red brick, and every house had its little railed garden before its doors and its green venetian blinds over its windows.

The portion of open land given up to the equestrians was precisely the site on which the demolished houses and the Old Town Hall had stood. It shelved down to a "flash"—a sheet of water occupying about a hundred acres—that had been formed by the subsidence of the soil. The surface of the field was singularly furrowed, as though at intervals a plough had been run through it. This open space grew but scanty, and that, coarse grass, and had the look as though blighted. It had been covered with buildings for half a century, and now that the buildings were demolished, it had not sufficiently recovered to resume its aspect of verdant meadow.

Elsewhere, proximity to water would have produced luxuriant vegetation. It was not so here. What grass there was seemed to be dead, the bushes were stunted, and the trees were mere skeletons devoid of leafage. In all directions were strewn torn sardine cases, open empty tins of Ramornie beef, broken marmalade pots, scraps of newspaper, scale from brine pans, decaying rabbit skins, corroded saucepans and perforated kettles, mutton bones, old boots that seemed to have been exploded by dynamite, toothless hair-combs of imitation horn, and from the branches of a dead tree swung an abandoned crinoline, which, having gone out of fashion, had there committed suicide.

The erection of the circus was complete, and highly-coloured pictures representing the troupe performing their most remarkable achievements were displayed in front of it. There was to be a procession of the Queen of Love, drawn in a mother-o'-pearl shell by ostriches, with Cupid on the box. Wild Indians in moccasins, and with scalps flying at their girdles, were to hunt the buffalo. A horse rivalling that of Baron Munchausen would dance on a tea-table without disturbing the cups. The Pearl of the Indies, in the lightest of gauze drapery, would bound through a flaming hoop. Performing dogs would drink and smoke and play whist. The Modern Proteus would go through twenty transformations on horseback.

The "Tailor of Brentwood" was declared on the posters to be a screaming farce, certain to convulse the spectators. Finally, the entertainment would conclude with a grand, and gorgeous, and hitherto unequalled display of the Queen of Love receiving the homage of gods, men and beasts.

Never, within the memory of the oldest inhabitant, were such attractions offered to the inhabitants of Saltwich. The outside of the great tent was contemplated by the assembled crowd with mixed feelings. Some of the eminently serious, who had descended—ay, condescended—to look at the erections in the Old Field, felt that Dr Tallow must be indeed a giant in eloquence to contend with, and wrest from Signor Santi a congregation sufficient to fill the New Hall. They believed that they stood on the verge of a crisis, when a revolution threatened, if it were not imminent. Servant girls were asking leave to visit sick mothers. Boys were pretending to have influenza colds which would keep them from attendance at the New Hall. School children, instead of rushing home when class was dissolved, ran to the field to peer through the joints in the boarding round the arena, or to lose themselves in astonishment at the pictures displayed. The supremacy of the grave in Saltwich stood in jeopardy. The serious looked vastly serious. Their mouths went down at the corners, and their confidence sank to their boots. There would be no overflow at the New Hall. There would be backsliders—there was no possibility of captures; some who were infirm in their gravity would be seduced to see the show, and all who might be "brought in" would, to a man, be in the sixpenny seats at the circus. But that was not all. Father and mother could not go together to listen to Dr Tallow, and leave their children at home, for how could they be sure that their little ones would not forsake their beds and steal away to the Old Hall Field? What missionary boxes would be safe when the fingers of domestics were itching for the money that would entitle them to see dancing dogs, acrobats and ostriches in procession? How could a serious husband be sure, suppose he left his wife behind to keep guard, that she would not yield to the solicitations of the young people, lock the door and go off with them to the horsemanship? Or the sedate wife—how could she be certain, when her husband left her at home, under the pretext that he was going to hear the great Jericho preacher, how could she have any well-grounded confidence that he would not turn his back on the New Hall at the first corner, and be found applauding the damsel balancing herself on one toe, and roaring over the jokes of the clown? What seeds of revolt! What rifts in domestic confidence were like to ensue from this inauspicious arrival of Signor Santi with his troupe in Saltwich!

At a distance of a hundred and fifty yards from the circus and its satellite booths and tents stood a solitary van. It was large, it was long, and was gaily painted. It was carved with wonderful flourishes, all of which were gilt. It had glass windows, partly obscured by muslin blinds and by red curtains. A stove flue projected through the roof. From the door a set of four steps was let down to the level of the soil.

On the topmost of these steps, with her back to the door, sat a girl of seventeen; but she was small, childlike for her age, and looked younger by a couple of years. She was engaged in opening and eating walnuts. She was delicately formed and graceful, with flowing, golden hair that reached her waist, and very dark eyes and brows. The brows and lashes were, in fact, so dark that many a woman, certainly all of the serious persuasion, would be sure to assert that they were dyed. Had her eyes been blue or grey, then the brows and lashes might indeed have been justly taken to be artificially coloured, but they were not so in this case. Nature is always cunning in her harmonies; and the dark-brown eyes, with a golden sheen in the brown, admirably agreed with the still darker brown of the arched brows and the long lashes. The girl had a roguish look in her face, and dimples in both cheeks, but mainly in that on the left, for she had the trick of smiling more on one side than on the other. But though one side of her face might laugh more than the other, it was not so with the eyes, in both of which was an equally merry twinkle. The one-sidedness of her smile gave a peculiar archness and special drollery to her sunny face.

Standing in front of her, below the steps, looking at her as she ate, with wonder in his great blue eyes, was a youth of one-and-twenty, with very fair hair, an open face, an expression gentle, and without force and strong individuality. Indeed, it may be said that there lay an evidence of constitutional or impressed timidity in the tremulous mouth and the quivering eyes.

He did not speak; he contented himself with staring.

The girl did not resent observation. Every now and then she looked him full in the eyes. Then hers sparkled and the dimples formed in the slightly-flushed cheeks. Whenever she did this, the youth coloured to the roots of his fair hair, and lowered his eyelids abashed. After this silent homage had continued for some while, and the girl was tired of eating and being contemplated in mute admiration, though not tired of the homage, she said, glancing up slyly,—

"Are you fond of nuts?"

The young man started, alarmed at being addressed.

"Look," said she; "you shall share mine."

She took half a dozen, stepped down to him and

thrust them into his pocket. He caught his breath and staggered back. She resumed her seat on the steps, and continued eating.

"What! No teeth to crack them?" she said. "I will help you again!"

Then she removed the upper shells of three, and placed them in a row on the step at her feet. They were fresh, yellow as butter.

"You are good," said the young man, shuffling from one foot to another; "but I will not deprive you of them."

He looked at the tempting nuts. He dared not put his hand so near her as to take one.

"Will you have one peeled?" asked the girl, flashing a glance at him, and puckering her funny little mouth.

Without awaiting a reply, she put a nut in her mouth, cracked the shell, then set to work deftly to remove the bitter skin. When the kernel was completely stripped, with a roguish look and her head a little on one side, and the golden hair flowing over one shoulder, she held out her palm, pink as a fan-shell, and with the kernel in it, white as an almond.

The boy recoiled in alarm.

"What! Do you think I am giving you poison? Oh, silly Adam! I am not Eve offering the forbidden fruit. This is quite harmless. There is no ban on walnuts. I thought you liked them—you looked at me in such a manner while I ate. Come! take and eat, you silly goose!"

Shyly the youth drew near, his face burning, his eyes on the ground, and his limbs trembling. He took the kernel so clumsily from the little, rosy palm that he touched the hand. A shock ran through him, and he gasped as though he had dipped his head under water.

"I thank you," he said.

"Why are you afraid of me? I am a teeny-weeny mite; you are a mighty fellow. Adam—"

"My name is not Adam, but Andrew."

"Andrew, if I were to put a walnut between my lips, and bid you come up close and bite it away, I believe you would die of terror."

He could not speak—the proposal made him giddy.

"No; but for all that I will not give you the chance. Take your three nuts, you toothless creature."

"I am ashamed; you have already put some in my pocket."

"You blush like a girl. We folks always give that we may take. I want something of you."

"What is that?"

"I want to know your thoughts. What were you thinking about me? What ideas were slouching about in that stupid head of yours covered with such a shock of tow, as you looked at me eating my walnuts?"

"I was thinking how pretty you were."

He reeled as he said this, astonished at himself for having paid a compliment.

The girl burst into a merry laugh and clapped her hands.

"We are getting on; this is famous. And your wishes—what are they? To come to the show and see me in all my glory—the Queen of Love? Well—it costs sixpence for the inferior seats; reserved seats, one shilling."

"I don't know—I am engaged."

"Engaged elsewhere? Where to?"

He hung his head.

"What a funny place this Saltwich is," said the girl.

"Saltwich funny! It is a very serious place. There are seven chapels in it of different denominations, besides—"

"Save me from the besides. I mean how funny it is that the place should live and thrive on salt."

"Yes—if there were no brine springs here, Saltwich would be nowhere; it has no other manufacture."

"How do you make salt?"

"We boil the brine."

"Where does the brine come from?"

"From the bowels of the earth."

"I should like to see salt made."

"Then," answered the young man eagerly, "come to the works to-morrow and I will show you everything."

"What are you?"

"A waller."

"What! a mason?"

"No; a waller with us means a boiler. I am on the day shift, and have to steam the brine, and rake the salt off as it forms."

"You are on the day shift?"

"Yes—I do not work at night."

"Then your objection falls through. You are *not* engaged. You will come to the show."

"It is not at the works that I am engaged," said the youth, colouring; "I have to go with my father to a meeting at the Town Hall."

"What! to the undenominational hop folks talk of as likely to spoil our attendance?"

"It is not a hop."

"What else can draw folks away? It must be a dance; that is the only other attraction I can think of that would take away the people from us. I suppose you Saltwichers love a hop. So would I if I had the chance—which I have not."

"You do not understand. If I could but persuade you to come to the meeting; it would do you so much good."

"I can't—I am engaged—in reality engaged. You can see that on the posters. Come and see me in my cockle-shell. Have you sixpence? No," said she, correcting herself; "from you I will have more—a shilling—and will reserve you the very best seat of all. Will you have the place? Give me the shilling."

"Here."

He extended a silver coin.

"And here in return is a ticket. Now, you must and shall come. It will be a grand show—it will be worth a bob to see me alone. I shall go about on two cream horses. I shall jump from the back of one to the back of the other, and all the while I shall look about for you. We have to keep very steady heads when we are performing, or dreadful things may happen."

"What things?"

"If I am not thinking of what I am about, but thinking of you, and why you have not come, then, there is no saying, I may drop between the horses, and go under their cruel hoofs, and there would be the end of poor little Queenie!"

The thought that this girl would be concerned if he did not appear, that his absence might set her little heart in a flutter of disappointment, was too much for the lad. He put his hands to his head—it was spinning like a teetotum; then she spread out her arms, shaking the broken nuts over the side of the steps.

"What is your name?" she asked.

"Andrew Grice."

"And I am Queenie Sant," said she. Then putting her head on one side, and throwing a mischievous twinkle into her eyes, she said coaxingly—"You will come and see me? Promise, you good Andrew, and I swear—"

"Hush, hush!"

"I vow and protest I will transform grave Andrew into a very merry Andrew; also, I will come to your salt works to-morrow. If I do not see you I will not come."

Then all at once a young man of rough exterior, with a shock of sandy hair on his head, strode to the side of the girl, and before she was aware, had bowed and lightly kissed her cheek. Turning to Andrew he said scornfully,—

"Stoop, fool, and pick up the nutshells offered; I, as a man, take what I can snatch, unasked—I—Rab Rainbow."

CHAPTER IV.

RAB RAINBOW.

THE girl sprang to her feet alarmed, incensed. The act of Rab Rainbow was so unexpected. Indeed, she had not even perceived the approach of the man. Nor had Andrew Grice observed him, so engrossed had he been in watching the circus girl, though Rab had been there for some little while, leaning his elbow against the van, with his fingers thrust through his light, bushy hair, looking down on the little Queen as she played with, and attracted the young waller.

The moment she had recovered herself, she sprang through the door into the caravan, and bolted it behind her.

Rab laughed, and cast himself carelessly on the steps, planting a foot on the ground on each side beyond the steps, thrust his rough cloth cap to the back of his head, and picked up such nuts as were not broken, and such fragments of kernel as lay on the step where he sat, ready for consumption.

Andrew Grice thought it incumbent on him to remonstrate with Rab for what he had done. Rainbow broke a nutshell, looked up, and asked contemptuously,—

"What brings you among the tents of the ungodly?"

"I can go where I please," retorted the waller, "without asking your leave."

"What will the daddy say?"

"I am my own master."

"No, you ain't, or weren't. I am surprised to see you among the good-for-naughts, and larking wi' circus-girls. You, Andrew, oh fie!"

"I was not larking."

"Quite right. You haven't the spring and carol of a lark in you."

Rab Rainbow was a tall, strongly-built young man, with light hair, and features of no regularity of shape, and no special character, but he had a pair of good, clear, grey eyes. He was dressed in a sandy suit, short cut, untidy but not ragged, bulged and patched, and on his legs were breeches and gaiters. The coat was dragged out of shape at the pockets, which were obviously often burdened with heavy weights, or distended beyond their proper size.

There was a careless good-nature in the man's face,

and this was all that was attractive about it; for he was far from handsome in feature, and his complexion was coarse and red. A gamekeeper would at once have set him down for a poacher, and, in fact, Rab's principal employment and amusement consisted in snaring rabbits and shooting pheasants in Delamere Forest. This royal forest at one time extended over 10,000 acres, but is now reduced to half that size. There are numerous noblemen's seats in the neighbourhood with extensive preserves. Five thousand acres of woodland, beside parks and preserves, afforded quite sufficient scope for Rab and those of his trade to pick up a livelihood. The poulterers' shops at Northwich, Saltwich and Winsford were kept supplied with game of all sorts by these free sportsmen.

"It would do you good, Andrew, to come to the circus to-night, and, as you've bought a ticket, come."

"I don't know. I am—"

"Yes; I know. The old 'Hammer' will take you with him to the undenominational affair. I wouldn't go, if I was you. I'd come here. You've bought a ticket; it's a sin to waste a shillin'. I know, and you know, just exactly what the American doctor will say. There'll be so many anecdotes, so many illustrations, so much butterin' of the grave, and so much damning of the gay. I've gone through that sort of thing scores of times, and so have you. I hate it. You won't have the chance of horsemanship every week, and you can get serious flummery any day."

"You should not speak thus," said Andrew, indignantly. "If you are a backslider, you need not throw your taunts at those from whom you've slipped away, and who stand where you fell."

"Yes," said Rab, thrusting his cap further back on his head, "I am a backslider, sure enough. I dare say I'm a worse man for it; I ain't sure I'm a better. But one thing I do know—I'm a truer man now than I was when I was kickin' in your net."

"That is because you were never radically and sincerely serious."

"May be," said Rab, with a shrug of one shoulder.

"I don't think these travelling horsemanship people ought to be encouraged," said Andrew. "That is why I don't patronise the show."

"Why should they not be encouraged?" asked Rainbow. "Don't you think life wants a little of the salt o' mirth strewn over it to make it taste less flat, and to keep it wholesome? May be they are just as useful in their way as are you wallers in your fashion."

"Anyhow, they are generally known to be a disreputable set."

"That's known to you, then, which is hid from me," said Rab, drawing his feet up on the step, and folding his arms on his knees. "Look here! You've been talkin' to the little lass in here, behind"—he pointed with his chin over his shoulder—"Do you know that she is the daughter of the manager? Do you think he ain't got fatherly love and care for her? Rats and mice have it for their little uns. Crows and jackdaws have it for theirs. You don't allow that mountebanks have what you know the beasts and birds possess. That never enters your serious noddle. You don't think that the Signor, as a father, would guard his child from every mischief, and eat his heart out with grief if ill came to the pretty mite? No; that never struck your dull imagination. And the young woman that goes through the fiery hoop, and dances on one toe on horseback—you mayn't suspect she's the wife of the clown, but I tell you she is so. If you'll come this evenin' and look at him instead of her, you'll see him wince every time she goes through the flames, and that he has his eye followin' her, and hands ready to catch her should she fall, all the while that he is crackin' his jokes and makin' grimaces, and cuttin' antics. If you'll come and see that, then you'll learn more of human nature than you will under the Rev. Tallow. And somethin' more you may learn—or, at least, come to suspect—that the clown would not have his wife, for all her muslin skirts and bare arms, do anything but what is fittin' and decent in an honest wife and a good mother. You'll rub your eyes when you've learnt that; and that's what you won't get at the New Town Hall."

"I am very rejoiced to hear this," said Andrew.

"I'll tell you somethin' more," said Rab. "These poor creatures in the circus, they paint for an hour, and then wash it all off, and they are natural men and women, as God made them, for the other twenty-three hours. There's folks—I name no names—as wouldn't set their foot inside the hossmanship, who paint, and never get out of paint. They eat in paint, they sleep in paint, they talk and they walk in it. And the coorious sarcumstance is, that everyone else sees it is paint but themselves. There be some such in your show—I don't say all—and the thing that's remarkable about it is, that in your show everyone paints up to deceive his own self first, and he does it thoroughly. That paint, red-lead, gets into the veins and colours his blood; that paint, white-lead, gets into the head and is converted into brain. I'll tell you what is the great difference between these horsemanship folk and those I speak of—the real difference that goes to the bottom of all. Those who paint in your show deceive themselves first, and then, when that is thoroughly accomplished—with a deception never to be shaken off—then they take in others. The fellows in the circus paint, and they never—not for one moment — deceive either themselves or others."

"I don't understand you."

"Don't you? I don't suppose you do. I'll tell you what the symptoms are. The fellows in your show get to so believe in and worship their own painted-up and false selves, that they think and say that nobody can be right unless he be a reflection of themselves. If they likes beefsteak puddin', then cursed be he who has a fancy for mutton hash. If they walk on the shady side of the street, then may a sunstroke take him who prefers to go on the south side. They have such a likin' for the smell of a cauldron of biled cabbage, that anathema be to him who likes the scent of the flowering beanfield."

"I'm not one of that sort," said Andrew, sharply.

"Ain't you? You're on the highway to it—what did you say just now about these poor horse-riders being a disreputable lot? You have been galled when on horseback yourself, I suppose, and so cannot allow anyone to be respectable who can ride."

Andrew turned to go away.

Rab called after him,—

"I've not done with you yet."

Andrew halted and reluctantly looked back.

"You don't often hear what is the opinion formed of you in Heathendom, so it is well to get it when you can. We're a wicked lot, we are, in them red brick cottages, and a wickeder lot was turned out o' them that tumbled down. We talk and we laugh and we have our opinions. Whether they be right or wrong, that's for such to say who holds the balances. I've been about in all coorses of life and conditions of men, and my notion is, there's a deal more good everywhere than you serious ones suppose, and there's good just where you don't expect to find it. Human natur' ain't all perfection in Jewry and all corruption in Heathendom. There are bad men, but the paint hides their badness, who'll be tonight gesticulatin' and haranguin' with the Rev. Tallow, and there'll be good and true men and women looking on at the horse-riders, ay, and ridin' the horses too! The human conscience is healthy and sturdy enough, and the fault I find with your Doctor Tallow and the likes of him is, they don't let it alone, but go pricking and poking at it, and whipping up a lather about it like them cuckoo-spittle insects on the young shoots in spring."

Andrew walked away.

Rab looked after him with a smile in his grey eyes.

"The chap ain't bad if let alone," said he.

As he sat, still smiling and looking after the retreating figure of the young waller, cautiously the window above his head was opened from within, without turning the door on its hinges; then a delicate arm was thrust out and took up Rab's cap from his head, so lightly, so gently, that he was hardly aware of the theft. He put up his hand and rubbed his head, looked about, saw no one, felt behind him, thinking the old bit of headgear had slipped down; then the cap was dropped on his rough locks again, and pinned into the side was a yellow rose.

CHAPTER V.

"HAMMER" GRICE.

ANDREW walked home slowly and thoughtfully. He had been brought up in the straightest sect of serious-mindedness; his world had been one overcast by clouds, through which flashed no sun to throw the ripple of life into sparkle and laughter. He had been shown mankind as sharply cleft into two spheres, two camps—that of the good and that of the bad—ever at war, sometimes in active hostility, sometimes with that army to which he belonged drawn within Torres Vedras lines, prepared for attack, awaiting the opportunity of taking the field. Such a view of mankind as this is one which commends itself easily, readily, to such as are children in years, and to those whose hearts never expand with the experience of life. They have no idea of the blending of tints; the doctrine of equations is beyond the grasp of their intellects. It is a view which has been formulated into a dogma. Men grow to manhood, and pass through life and descend into their graves, possessed with the idea that their fellow-men are capable of broad and decided classification—into two hosts ranged against each other in internecine strife; into two states, in which the one is of light, the other of darkness. Humanity may be actually of one blood, but it is not, it never was, of one spirit. Not Adam and Eve, bound in mutual sympathies and loving each other to death, are the parents of the human race, but Cain and Abel, envying, hating, pursuing one another. Humanity is not, as a rule, penetrated by like emotions, moved by like ambitions, is not equally subject to caprices. It is not at one time prone to strive after high ideals, and then to sink to basenesses; not to be now generous and then mean; now brave and then cowardly; now true and then false. Far from it! All the loftiness, generosity, heroism, truth are to be found in the one army; and all the baseness, meanness, cowardice, falsehood in the other; and should there appear in that other some tokens of what is accounted noble, and great, and liberal, then these are not to be accounted in them as intrinsic virtues, but to be esteemed as affectations and unsubstantial phantasms.

Teaching such as this is at home under the turban as well as under the triple tiara; it nestles into the heart under the Pharisee's phylactery and the preacher's gown; it is a teaching which accommodates itself to every creed and confession.

Jabez Grice was dominated by this teaching. It did not tincture merely, it constituted the very essence of his convictions; it petrified them to adamant, and rendered them as immutable as the rules of Nature. Jabez, or "Hammer" as he was commonly designated, had reared his son Andrew, a pliant youth, in this same aspect of life. Sometimes such teaching supplies to a naturally feeble character that iron which it lacks, but at other times it has a debilitating tendency, and takes the lime out of the bones.

"Hammer" Grice occupied a house in a new row of cottages on a ridge of rising sandstone that ran no risk of settlement, and looked down with a frown on Heathendom. It was tenanted by exemplary individuals, all serious. No. 4 in Alma Terrace (Jewry, such was its slang designation) was the dwelling that was occupied by Jabez Grice.

From the height of Jewry the very serious sent forth skirmishing parties to hold street preachings in Heathendom, with the hope—a forlorn one—of effecting captures. But these parties rarely returned with spoils; they were usually followed by a groaning, cat-calling mob.

Heathendom retaliated by suborning men with barrel-organs, that ground off dance tunes, to perform along the length of Alma Terrace, and it sent forth its boys and girls to caper and waltz to these strains, under the horrified windows of Jewry.

Every available engine to annoy or discomfit Heathendom was set in operation by the very serious who, being the respectable, the monied and well-conducted of Saltwich, had the command of the forces that could be employed against the disreputable, impecunious and noisy. They had them watched by the police; they harried them through the School Attendance Committee; they visited them through the Sanitary Officers; they had them dropped upon by the Excise; they worried them through the rate-collectors. They made it impossible for a son or daughter of Heathendom to escape into respectability through any other door than that of the chapel. Should a young man from this quarter desire a situation in the police, or as a keeper, or in the army, or navy, no respectable man in the superior quarter would give him a character; and no girl had a chance, for the same reason, of obtaining a situation in a reputable house.

Saltwich was a town that had started up in the extensive parish of Scatterley, with a church at a distance of two miles. The Vicarage was occupied by a gentle, timid man, fond of collecting moths, an authority on lepidoptera, unable to cope with the difficulties of his position, and without the moral energy to attempt to do so. A good, kind man; but rather scientific than spiritual. He hunted beetles and moths, rather than souls. He was content, in face of the dominant nonconformity, to be left unmolested to minister to a couple of farmers, a sporting squire, and his own family. No man was of less account in Saltwich than the Vicar of Scatterley; and even had those whom Jewry had banned appealed to him for encouragement, he would not have dared to uphold them, lest, by so doing, he should offend the nonconformists, and the Serious-Minded of all denominations should conspire against him, and wrest from him one of the two farmers to whom he still ministered on sufferance. Over against the Reverend Edward Meek stood the layman, Jabez Griçe, the most commanding power in Saltwich. He was not a man of means or of position. He was foreman at Brundrith's Salt Works on a salary of forty shillings a week, but he was a man of an intense and aggressive personality.

Giants are not necessarily great men, nor are mighty men always big in size. A man is not to be measured by the number of stones he weighs, and the number of feet and inches he stands. "Hammer" Grice was of moderate size, solid in structure, and with a firm head planted on a short neck and broad shoulders. He was not contained within the clothes that enveloped him. He filled every room he entered, he filled his own house, he filled all Jewry; it may almost be said that he filled all Saltwich. Certainly no man in that brine-pumping and steaming town had anything approaching his power. In the factory he was greater than Brundrith. In political influence he was a greater man than the Member of Parliament; in chapel, pastor and elders were his humble servants. No committee could be formed without Grice in it, and, when in it, the fellow-members did little else than register the opinions and resolutions of "Hammer." At an election he swept votes together with an irresistible force; on a platform he could sway his hearers and make them think and feel with himself. He was not an educated man, nor a logical reasoner. He carried his audience with him, not so much by argument as by assertion. No antagonist answered him with impunity. He crushed him under facts, or, at least, statements, or withered him with his scorn.

He was a man who never hesitated in the formation of an opinion, and who never wavered, when once his opinion was formed.

Andrew, brought up under this man, of an amiable, pliable disposition, was bent and moulded as his father desired. He saw, heard, felt through his father's organs. His father could not be wrong in his estimates, and could do no wrong. The strength of the superior nature, instead of infusing its vigour into the inferior, sucked from the latter what little force it possessed.

But Andrew had reached that age when the sap of youth is most vigorous, and he now, for the first time, began to be conscious of, and to feel impatience at, the restraints that had been put upon him, and which he had worn without a murmur as a child. He thrust from him Rab's sneers at the insincerity of "Hammer" and his colleagues. Andrew knew his father, and knew that he was genuine to the core. There was no question as to his earnestness. That Jabez Grice was one of those who imposed on himself before imposing on others, or who imposed on others because he first thoroughly imposed on himself—this was an innuendo of Rab's not worthy of consideration.

But there was something in what Rab had said relative to the vagabond troupe that had stuck in the mind of Andrew, and the poacher's words had fallen—come apt—on thoughts forming in the brain of the young man during his conversation with the Queen of Love.

He had been drawn against himself into this conversation. He had stood looking at the girl, wondering at her beauty, and, in his own mind, marvelling that the Creator should have sent such a creature into the world to run to inevitable wreckage. Then, whilst these thoughts were turning in his head, the girl had begun to notice him, and had lured him on, with cleverness and coquetry, into buying a ticket for the performance. She had some self-respect, some grace in her, for she had resented the impudence of Rab Rainbow, had flushed with shame and had fled from his advances. When the girl had disappeared, then the poacher had spoken with him, and had said words which, if true, were a revelation, such as is wrought by the rending of clouds, and the display of a horizon illumined by sunshine and radiant with colour.

Was it possible that the daylight was not confined to Goshen, but was diffused also throughout Egypt? Was it possible that the dew of heaven fell on the herb of the field and forest as well as on cabbages and Brussels-sprouts? Was it possible that there was sweetness of song, and simplicity of life, and harmony of plumage in the wild bird of the air, as well as in the caged canary and the fowls in the poultry-house? As Andrew walked from the Old Hall Field, he saw an Italian playing a hurdy-gurdy, with a monkey, dressed in trousers and a scarlet coat, running up the blighted tree, swinging in the wires of the discarded crinoline, then, at a word from his master, taking a tray and going round soliciting coppers. Andrew cast in a trifle; but, as he did so, a spring of gall welled up in his heart. Had he not been reared by his father much as this monkey had been trained by the Savoyard? He had been taught to foot it to his father's piping; he was held by him, chained from going his own way; he was bidden by him do this and leave that, and he had no option in any matter, and, even as this monkey, he was sent round with missionary boxes and collecting cards. His brow coloured, and he turned quickly away. He became conscious of straitness, and, for the first time in his life, was inclined to strain his muscles and snap the bandages that were wrapped and knotted about him.

He had been a good boy—diligent in his work, regular in his hours, quiet in the house, docile before his father, and affectionate to his aunt who lived with his father, kindly, obliging to all. He had tasted nothing more stimulating than ginger-beer, had heard nothing more mirth-provoking than a humorous discourse at a chapel anniversary; the social gatherings which he had frequented had been all within the precincts of the Tabernacle or Temperance Hall. He had read nothing more exhilarating than a missionary magazine. Although living in a world in which the knowledge of good and evil (mainly the latter) is pretty generally diffused, and is acquired without the institution of Board Schools, yet Andrew was singularly guileless—as white in mind as blameless in conduct—so completely had he been kept, or had kept himself, within the circle of the serious. Now manhood was reached, and with manhood came a consciousness of innate power, a craving for independence. The imagination of Andrew began to plume its wings, his will to stiffen itself, and his mind to harbour the thought that it was not well for him always to live in abject subserviency, even to so admirable a father as was his.

On reaching No. 4 Alma Terrace, Andrew knew at once that his father was at home, by the fumes of tobacco that met him as he opened the door. He found "Hammer" seated by the fire reading his paper. Jabez recognised his son's footsteps, but did not trouble to look up, nor did he remove his pipe from his lips to throw him a greeting. Why should he? They worked in the same factory. Jabez was not one to trouble himself about the amenities of life; he contented himself with what was practical, substantial.

Andrew saw that the table was laid, and he put his hand upon it. In so doing, he threw down a fork.

"Now then, clumsy!" called Jabez, without raising an eye from the line he was reading.

Andrew stooped to pick up the fork, and, in setting it on the table, rattled the cups.

The father growled.

"I should like a word, father, if disengaged."

"I am here."

"I have been to the Old Hall Field. They are there."

"Who are the *They* that are there?"

"The circus people. They have set up their tents.'

"We sent them to the Old Hall Field," said Jabez.

"It is going to be an unusually good horsemanship."

"Possibly."

"I am fond of horses."

"Horses are one thing. Legs and muslin skirts are another."

"Father, I do not think I shall be able to accompany you to the New Hall to-night."

"Indeed."

Jabez did not raise his eyes from the paper, but Andrew saw his fingers clench the sheet more tightly, and heard him snort.

"I have so often attended this sort of thing," said Andrew.

"You have never heard the Rev. Tallow."

"No; but I have heard the female revivalist, and the negro evangelist, and the pugilistic apostle, and—"

"And what?"

"It's always very much the same. I don't feel any call to hear Tallow."

"Well—what more?"

The words fell from Jabez like lumps of iron.

"Well, father, and I thought—as a bit of a variety, and as, somehow, I have got a ticket for a reserved seat—that—that I'd go to the circus to-night."

"So you are going to the circus?"

"You don't very much mind, father, do you?"

"And where will you go after the circus?"

"Well—I shall be home as soon as you."

"You will not come home at all."

A pause, during which the frizzle of frying onions in the kitchen could be heard. There was to be beefsteak for supper. The smell of the onions mingled with the smoke of tobacco.

"This is what I mean," said Jabez; "you ought before this to have taken lodgings where to stay. You do not stay here. This is not a house in which frequenters of circuses can sit down with chapel-goers. A house divided against itself, No. 4 Alma Terrace shall never be. I give you till half-past seven to remove your clothes. If every rag is not gone by half-past seven, I chuck what remains into the street. Bethulia! dish up!"

"Father, do you mean to turn me out?"

"He that heareth not the Church, let him be to thee as a heathen man and a publican."

"But, father, that's different. Do you mean to say you are the Church?"

"Yes, I am; what else is the Church?" Jabez put down the paper. "Dish up the steak and onions sharp, Bethulia. I'm hungry!"

CHAPTER VI.

THE CIRCUS.

Rab was in his place on a bench at the circus. He looked about him for Andrew, but could see him nowhere.

"I thought the fellow had hardly the dare in him," said Rab.

The benches filled rapidly. It was really questionable whether any would be left in Saltwich to sit under Dr Tallow, so numerous was the attendance at Signor Santi's rival entertainment.

One thing was, however, noticeable—that the reserved red baize-covered seats did not fill. A good deal of red baize was still exposed. Those who did speckle its surface were not Saltwichers, but country folk, the families of neighbouring gentry. They had sent their children with tutors and governesses, some had even come themselves. A rector was there with wife and offspring. A schoolmaster from a distance was there with his pupils.

THE CIRCUS

Cheshire is famous for its horses; its heart beats high at racing periods. It is in the full glow of life in the hunting months. There are studs around Delamere Forest. The very high roads are furnished with soft trotting ground at their sides specially adapted for horses taken out to practice. From the stables had come grooms and horseboys in great numbers. The exhibition was, above all others, calculated to interest and delight them. Some of the small shopkeepers of Saltwich were present; such, that is, as were not devoted hand and soul to the serious faction, and Heathendom, as far as its finances would admit, was there to man and boy.

The tent was sustained by a pole in the midst, around which hung a circular chandelier supporting oil lamps. The arena had been strewn with sawdust, which, being slightly damp, exhaled an odour that impregnated the atmosphere. The structure on which the public was to sit, raised stage on stage, was simple to rudeness. The deal boards employed had been as few as was consistent with safety. The whole fabric was temporary and flimsy, but was calculated to sustain any amount of direct pressure exerted vertically, when occupied by a crowd of spectators. The boards were not jointed, and there was no flooring under the benches, consequently men who incautiously thrust their hats under their seats, or women their baskets of provisions, had them precipitated to the turf below. A mother screamed because her child had dropped into space, but it was recovered uninjured, having been caught by its frock. There was an outcry from a woman who, in counting her change, had emptied the contents of her purse over the benches and sixpences were dancing down the stage, and threepenny bits slipping between the joints. Some merriment was provoked by a Scatterley farmer who, on taking his place, removed and looked into his hat It was surmised that he thought he was in church, and that he was saying his prayers.

Vendors went round with oranges and buns; gingerbeer bottles popped and squirted their contents into faces and over frocks.

Personal observations were made on all sides, as was inevitable in a place where everyone knew everyone else.

"My word! There's Susan Naylor in a new bonnet. Who ever is that with her? She's surely not picked up a fresh young man?"

"Well, I declare, if that isn't Tommy Tinker! And he is in arrears at the shop. He might have paid for his 'backy, and stayed away."

"There are all the Suggars. Their business must be flourishing. Three whole tickets and eight children at half-price. That makes five-and-six. I'm astonished they ain't ashamed to show what profits they make out of us labouring people."

THE CIRCUS

"Well, I never! There's the Townsends in the reserved seats. What swells they are become! What makes them strut such peacocks is, that they have come in for their uncle's money. But they'll soon run through that if they go reserved-seating it every day!"

"Why, surely the Linterns ain't gone to the sixpenny places, and they gave champagne at their daughter's wedding! I call that shabby—worse than shabby; it's positively dirty. I'd stay away, or go reserved if I gave champagne at a wedding."

The arena was not perfectly smooth. It had been brushed over more than once, but now a sort of ripple was observable on the surface of the sawdust. The manager noticed this and summoned a couple of workmen in white jackets to sweep the arena once more.

When they had withdrawn, in leaped the clown with his familiar "Here we are again, and how are you, ladies and gentlemen, and all the little ones at home?"

He was greeted with applause and laughter.

The usual dialogue ensued between him and the manager, who cracked his whip, and made the clown jump and rub his shins. It was really astonishing to the spectators how little the jokes of the clown affected the manager. He spoke without a muscle moving; there seemed to be in him neither a sense of humour nor a spark of compassion. He laughed at no sally, and spared no stroke of the lash.

Then entered the little Queen of Beauty, as advertised, in her mother-o'-pearl shell drawn by ostriches. The birds and carriage were not by any means equal to what the public had been led to anticipate from the flaming posters. The ostriches were ruffled and frowsy; they wore a distressed air, and walked in ungainly fashion. The car was conspicuously of pasteboard covered with silvered paper, and somewhat battered. But the little Queen herself surpassed all that had been promised. She was clothed in white muslin, had a wreath of stars about her head, and held a star-tipped sceptre in her hand. Her golden hair flowed over her fair shoulders in waves of sunlight; her complexion, perhaps heightened artificially, was brilliant; brighter than stars shone her merry eyes, full of light though dark in colour.

Rab set his cap on his head, with the yellow rose in front. The Queen was greeted with thunders of applause, a portion of which was contributed by Rab, who stamped and roared, and clapped his hands, till his face was red with exertion.

As the Queen made the circuit of the arena, her eyes roamed over the benches, and a smile lighted her cheerful face. When her eye rested on the young poacher, he flattered himself that she made him a slight inclination of her sweet head, that a brighter or more roguish twinkle kindled her eye, and that the dimples of her cheek deepened with a truer smile than that which had been accorded to the general public.

After that the Queen had retired as she came, Rab saw little of what followed. He was consumed with impatience for the reappearance of the Queen of Love and Beauty. The buffalo hunt passed before him unheeded. He hardly saw the wild Indians. He cared not for the performing dogs of the clown, nor for that buffoon's jests and capers. His eyes were riveted on the door through which the little Queen had disappeared, and through which she was to return. When the curtains of the entrance were raised and a horse issued forth, he hoped it might be that she was to mount, but when some one else— an athlete in fleshings, throwing balls and waving flags—leaped upon the sawdust, and with a skip was on the saddle, then Rab uttered a dissatisfied growl.

Andrew was not there—Andrew who had been specially invited; Andrew, who had been privileged to hold converse with the little fairy, who had been offered peeled kernels in her delicate palm, on whom words of favour and beaming smiles had been lavished —Andrew Grice was not there. Where was his heart? Was he a man of stone? Had he in his composition neither pluck nor gallantry?

If the Queen had offered Rab her empty nutshells, he would have worshipped her hand. If she had invited him to come, he would have spent his last farthing to be present. And this fellow Andrew, had she not told him she desired his attendance, that she would look out for him with her bright eyes; that, were he to disappoint her, it might even cause her to fall from horseback?

Rab's cheeks glowed. He swore, if he saw Andrew, he would beat him for disappointing that little heart. And yet he was glad Andrew was not there. Had young Grice been on the bench, then, perhaps, on him would have fallen the eyes of the little Queen; to him would have been accorded the nod and smile, and he himself, poor Rab, would have been disregarded. The rose that Queenie had given him, Rab had placed in water till the moment he went to the show then he had donned it with pride, in the hopes, that were not blighted, that by it the pretty circus girl might recognise him.

Rab's thoughts were diverted from their current—something was wrong. What was it that engaged the attention of the manager? He was pointing to the central pole, and had summoned the white canvas-jacketed men. The pole was not as it had been set. It was inclined so that the circle of lights touched it on one side. The workmen drove wedges between the base and the soil, and so restored it to uprightness.

Meanwhile Signor Santi amused the spectators by an interlude—an exhibition of the sagacity of his famous Arab mare, Black Bess. He made her leap a five-barred gate, he bade her dance on her hind legs; he summoned her to him, and she came, docile as a lamb. He bade her kneel and throw herself on her side and simulate death, whilst he fired a pistol over her head. Bess knelt as required, but tossed her head, snuffed the soil, threw herself down indeed, but, instead of lying prostrate and tranquil, reared herself to her knees, then sprang up again.

"Bess! What is this? I never knew you disobedient before. Down, Bess!"

Santi cracked his whip. The Arab hesitated, trotted away, came back, pawed the soil, snuffed at it once more, went down on her knees, but again sprang to her four feet and stood before her master, trembling, sweating and snorting.

Nothing would induce her now to go through her performance; neither threat nor persuasion were of avail, and Santi was forced to dismiss her to the stable.

"Ladies and gentlemen, I never knew Bess like this before. Something has alarmed her. Perhaps the workmen driving the wedges. We will find other animals more tractable."

He cracked his whip, fired the pistol into the air, and in bounded a pair of cream-coloured horses fastened together by their heads, with white and silver trappings on their backs.

In another moment the little Queen appeared dancing in, dressed in white muslin strewn with spangles, so that her every movement made her twinkle like a frosted bush on a sunny winter morning.

She ran to the horses, the clown offered a hand, and in a moment she was in the saddle of one, poised on a single foot, amidst the applause of the public, especially of Rab.

The manager cracked his whip and trailed the lash along the sawdust in a circle.

Suddenly, as by an enchanter's wand, absolute stillness was produced in that great concourse of spectators. Santi's arm was as though paralysed as he drew his whip along. The cream-white horses had recoiled; the clown, with his hands to his head, was looking, mouth open, at the chandelier.

The only sound heard was the straining and creaking of the timber structure occupied by the public, and the strain and creak were like those of a ship labouring in a heavy sea. Then ensued the tinkle and crash of the lamps that smote each other and went to pieces.

The hush was momentary, and then there rose a great burst of confused noises, first as a gasp, then as a roar. What ensued was a matter of a few moments only, though it may take a page in which to describe it.

The central tent pole was seen, in spite of the wedges, to lean, and then to be sinking into the earth. That this was the case was, however, hardly realised at once; it appeared as though the pole were collapsing telescopically. As it gave way, the vast stretch of canvas extended over the circus began to sag, to flap about and fall together. Simultaneously the lamps broke, some poured forth volumes of smoke; in others the light reached the oil, ignited it, exploded the receivers and poured down in liquid fire. The spectators on one side of the ring witnessed a strange phenomenon—they saw the other side lifted up as though a wave were passing under it, whilst those opposite were aware that the further side of the circus, with its benches and the occupants of those benches, was being swallowed up in the earth. The strain on the concentric rings of the structure was more than they could bear, the supports fell, the boards flipped out of their places, and the whole fabric began rapidly to go to pieces. Those spectators who occupied the highest benches were precipitated eight feet to the soil.

The barrier dividing the arena from the spectators was covered with crimson drapery; it was parted as though rent asunder by giant hands, and the drapery was torn across. A wave ran along the surface of sawdust from side to side, leaving a ripple, then the ripple changed into a rent, the earth gaped and the sawdust began to powder down into the fissure.

A north-west wind was blowing; it caught, bustled about the relaxed canvas, and breaking in through some of the gaps, assisted in the confusion by blowing out, or blowing to explosion, lamps hanging at the sides and hitherto unaffected, and by tossing the loose canvas against the benches over which it was falling, and sweeping from them the frightened people.

In a moment or two the whole fabric would be a wreck, a weltering mass of flapping canvas, dislocated boards, shrieking human beings, plunging horses, flaming oil and fluttering shreds of crimson baize. The terror was general. Men and women fought to escape, regardless of sex and relationship. They fell through the scaffolding; they beat at and tore a way through the exterior boarding. Screams, entreaties, curses blended with the crashing of timber, the snorting of horses, the bellowing of the bison, the yelp of dogs, the pistol-like reports of the tossed canvas, the crash of glass; these together formed a hubbub of sound, pierced at intervals by the shriller shriek of some lost and frightened child, shrill as the whistle of a locomotive.

Whether it were the vibration caused by the tramp of the horses, or the weight of such a multitude of spectators, or both combined, certain it was that the crust of earth that overlay a vacuum, caused by the exhaustion of the salt rock, had given way, as had previously other portions of the surface hard by, and the circus and the ground about it were going down into an unfathomed abyss.

CHAPTER VII.

RAB TO THE RESCUE.

WHEN the earth began to move, to slide from under their hoofs, the two cream-coloured horses linked together, had been thrown into a paroxysm of terror, had leaped, plunged and flung the little Queen, who fell before their heads, on the sawdust.

Rab saw her danger instantly, and without regarding anything else, without questioning what had caused the panic, beat his way with fists and elbows through the rings of spectators that intervened, and who were up and struggling to escape, and leaped the barrier to her rescue.

The confusion was general before he had reached the arena, and to the experienced eye of an inhabitant of the salt district, there could be no question as to what the phenomenon was that was wrecking the circus.

As Rab threw himself over the barrier, the manager, Santi, sprang at the heads of the horses. These beasts, in their terror, had managed to snap the thongs that arched their necks and restrained their motions, and now, with heads free, they were plunging, striving to tear themselves apart, and menaced the prostrate girl with their hoofs. Queenie was insensible. Rab caught her up in his arms, brushed back her golden hair to see that her face had not been trampled on, and then looked about to determine in which direction he was to escape with her. On all sides the spectators were flying; some were still on the benches, running this way and that, bewildered, unable to find the entrance; others had fainted, and hung insensible over the seats, but the greater number had got down to the level of the ground, and had found, or were forcing, their way out at the sides. The interior was now dark — dense with whirling volumes of petroleum smoke, shot through with red flames.

The performing dogs stood, one on a barrel, the other on the barrier of the arena, howling with fear. Rab could see that the cream-coloured horses had gained the mastery, and were dragging Santi, whose hand was entangled in the reins; that the central pole was coming rapidly down with all its broken lamps.

He could see the fissure in the arena widening, like a great mouth that was breaking into a laugh of mockery at the ruin and panic wrought.

Not a moment was to be lost. He could not tarry to

disengage the manager, nor reassure the clown, who, in abject terror, had crept into the barrel, where he was sobbing and beating his hands together. He looked about him, assured himself of the direction in which the earth was subsiding, and, bearing the unconscious girl in his arms, made for the further side of the arena. The rift in the soil was between him and the point he desired to reach, its ugly edges crumbling down into the depth, with now and then whole clots of earth and sawdust dropping in in a mass. It was uncertain whether the foot could find a hold to allow of a leap, and the soil be firm enough beyond to receive the feet without yielding. But there was no time available for measuring risks and calculating alternatives. Rab leaped the crack successfully, and reached the red-draped barrier precisely where one of the white performing dogs was perched, quivering with fear, and howling. At that same moment, down fell the awning, striking Rab, and precipitating him to the ground, throwing the dog down with him, and enveloping him, his senseless burden, and the wretched hound, in its cumbrous folds. For a moment or two Rab could not move, he was so weighed down and entangled with the canvas.

But Rab was a fellow of strength and energy. He laid his burden under the barrier which remained upright, and which, after a fashion, sustained the fallen awning, and, using both hands, with a knife hacked and ripped at the canvas. In places this had caught fire. It hung over the wrecked scaffolding, like skin on a wasted body, loose about the bones. It flapped in the wind. The air entered below at the torn sides and blew it out in bellies, then it collapsed again. Guys that had been ripped out of the earth, or torn, slapped the canvas, as though some one were lashing it with whips. In the arena it covered everything. The struggling horses were seen leaping under it, the lamps were burning their way through it; it began to sag down into the rift that was gradually widening, as though the earth, having opened her mouth, were mumbling and drawing in the cloth thrown over her face.

Rab left the still unconscious girl under the barrier that served to stay up the canvas, whilst he hacked with his pocket-knife, and tore with his hands at the smothering, all-enveloping cover. He speedily ripped a hole in it. At once the dog leaped on his shoulders and sprang through. Then he felt himself gripped at the heel, and, looking down, saw the painted face of the clown, who had crawled out of the barrel and wormed his way after him, with a dim instinct that by this means he could escape. The man was crying like a little child, and the tears had run the paint off his cheeks; as he wiped his face, he smeared red and black together, rubbed the artificial eyebrows into a tuft on his nose, and covered his white sleeve with stains.

"Help me, man!" said Rab. "Lay hold of that end of the rag."

"I can't do nothing, I'm so shook. Oh, my! is it the end of the world come? I'll be good. I'll promise to be good. I won't drink no more. I'll take the pledge."

"You fool! Stand on your feet and assist me."

"Oh! I can't! Is it the end of all things? If it is, I'll wear the blue ribbon. I will—I swear I will! I will! I will! Oh! I'll be so good! I'll read nothing but tracts."

"Out of the way! Do you see the little Queen there?"

"Is she dead also? Oh, dear! I'm not fit to die! I've been accustomed to shave on Sundays."

"Let go!" The clown had laid hold of Rab's shoulders, and was trying to climb on them so as to escape. "It's the end of nothing save your show, you selfish hound! Can't you help me with the little Queen?"

Rab tore the sailcloth apart. The fresh air blew in on him. Above was the vault of heaven strewn with ten thousand stars. He looked round a moment, scrambling up the canvas over part of the scaffolding that seemed secure. In places, flames were leaping, ghostlike, high in the air above the oil or canvas that was burning. The confused mixture of voices of those outside the heap of wreckage filled his ears—

the cries, shouts, objurgations, entreaties, orders, all mingled into a general roar. Outside, mothers who had escaped were seeking their children, strayed children were screaming for their parents, husbands called to their wives. Those spectators who had escaped were mingled with a crowd come down from the town to see the disaster and render help. They endeavoured to organise parties to search the wreck, and extricate such as were still buried, but no one was in authority, and none would obey self-constituted directors.

Some of the grooms and stable-boys had run to the subsidiary tent that served as green-room for the performers, and where also were those horses prepared to take part in the representation, and were assisting men in fleshings and velvet, the Signora Muslina in gauze skirts, and trapeze men half dressed, to lead away the animals. Wild Indians, talking cockney English, drove the ostriches before them; a mechanic had shouldered the mother-o'-pearl car, and was carrying it to a place of security. The buffalo was pawing the soil, bellowing, and would allow no one near him.

Rab now stooped and raised the red repp that covered the barrier. Queenie was still unconscious. He threw her over his left shoulder, and proceeded to thrust the coils of canvas under his feet and draw himself up to the surface. The clown persisted in dragging at him. He had lost all self-control, and was unnerved.

The course Rab had elected to take was by no means a safe one. He had to make his way over the fallen sailcloth that covered the scaffolding, some of which stood, some was down, and some was leaning and would yield with the least additional weight. Moreover, the wind under the canvas played with it, and made it most precarious where to tread.

"You go forward," said Rab to the clown, "straight as a line to where yon star shines afore your eyes, or as near a line as sarcumstances admit. Tread away, and I'll follow with my precious burden."

The white dog jumped about its fellow-performer and barked. The clown put down his hand and patted it.

"Glad you are saved, Tweedledum," said he. "P'r'aps it ain't so bad after all."

A shrill voice outside was heard calling,—

"Nelson! honey, dear! Nelson! where are you?"

"Coming! coming!" screamed the clown. Then turning his head over his shoulder, he said to Rab, "That's the signora. That's Mrs Nelson. She is seeking me."

A little more confidence came to the poor fellow as he heard the voices of the crowd, and, above all, that of his wife. He could not see the people, for the canvas inclined upwards to the boarded side of the circus that was not broken down. As he looked back, he saw behind him the burning mass, and, beyond that, all was blackness—everything had disappeared.

He stepped along. Perhaps it was his costume, the absurd tufts of hair on his head, the high rolls for epaulettes, the out-stuffed thigh pads, but his every attitude was grotesque. He could not put forward a foot to feel if the canvas before him would sustain his weight, but he made an antic, and, as he stepped along, he continued shouting,—

"I'm coming, my poppet! I'm coming, my honey! Your Nelson is safe!"

Rab thought he was playing the buffoon.

"Have done with your merry-Andrew tricks," said Rab. "This is no time for fooling!"

"I'm not fooling. I can't help it. I'm doing my best," protested the clown, and he groped along, with the dog dancing at his side. "Coming, poppet! Coming, sweetheart!"

Every step he took, every inhalation of pure air, every strident call from his still invisible wife, served to restore elasticity to the spirits of the clown, and recover his mind of the fears that had oppressed it. He stepped firmer. He beat his breast, and said,—

"I won't! I won't! No; I won't!"

"You won't do what?" asked Rab, treading at his heels.

"I won't take the pledge. I won't read tracts, and I'll shave just when it suits me—Sabbath included."

Then he reached the edge of the hoarding, looked over; a gas light illumined his face—some boys saw him and laughed.

'Here we are again!" shouted the man, and turned a somersault to descend to the crowd. "Poppet, here I am!"

Rab followed cautiously and descended slowly. He was greeted with questions, to none of which he replied, and with offers of assistance, none of which he accepted.

He worked his way with his right hand, thrusting men and women aside, till he got through the crowd. Then he made at once for the row of cottages entitled Heathendom, in one of which he lived along with his mother.

As he reached the door, the girl stirred on his shoulder, attempted to raise herself, and asked,—

"Father! where is father?"

"Lie quiet, little Queenie," said Rab. "My mother shall attend on you, and I will go back to look for your poor father."

"Who are you?"

"I am the chap to whom you gave the yaller rose. I'll do you no harm. Trust me."

CHAPTER VIII.

NUTS.

ANDREW was not prepared for open revolt against the authority of his father, nor was he ready to undergo major excommunication. In token that he gave way, he tore his ticket and threw the fragments into the fender, and his father accepted this act as one of tacit submission. But in heart Andrew was rebellious. "Hammer" believed that he had won a victory and riveted more firmly his domination over his son. He was mistaken; he had shaken his hold on the lad's conscience. The punishment threatened was out of all proportion to the offence. Andrew's conviction of the justice of his father had received a shock. He questioned his affection for him.

Andrew asked himself: Was a parent right in treating his son, when arrived at manhood, as the Savoyard treated his monkey? Was a monkey ordained by Nature to wear a red coat, to be controlled by a chain, to run up water-pipes, and hold out a begging-box? Would a monkey be justified *in foro conscientiæ* in breaking his chain, tearing off jacket and breeches, throwing aside his collecting box, and making for the greenwood? The man and the monkey do not stand to each other in the same relation as father to son. That made a difference. What was lawful in the monkey was, perhaps, not sufferable in the son. In that the monkey was a happier, more privileged being than Andrew. It might assert its liberty without conscientious twinges.

In another point the monkey stood higher in the scale of happiness than Andrew. It was allowed to run and jump; it might stand on its head and stretch its little feet to heaven. It might dance and make grimaces; it might take without scruple anything—nuts—nuts!—(Andrew's breath came quick)—anything offered it. It was not obliged to go through the routine of missionary, temperance and undenominational as well as sectarian meetings.

Andrew had been eating his portion of beefsteak and fried onions. He laid down his fork, and lapsed into a brown study.

"What is up, Andrew?" asked his father.

"I was thinking," answered the youth submissively.

"Thinking of what?"

"Only that monkeys don't have—taking all into consideration—such a bad time of it."

His father stared, then turned to Beulah, his sister, and said,—

"I shall be on the platform. I suppose I shall be forced to say a few words."

"Oh, brother, of course, of course! What would the meeting be without an address from you?"

"I'll do what is right," said "Hammer," bringing his fist down on the table. "I'll do it, even though the Philistines be encamped against me with their host in battle array."

"The Philistines will not be there, brother."

"You are right, Beulah, they will not. They will be down at the Old Hall Field, with skipping ropes and butterflies and all the pomps! I'll speak to-night!"

"You always do, father," said Andrew.

"I do, yes!" answered Jabez. "Because I always do what I ought to do. Time is up. Get ready at once."

He rose from table, without looking to see whether his sister and son had finished their meal; he ordered the table to be cleared. Then he remembered that he had not shaved, fetched hot water, and spent a quarter of an hour in polishing his upper lip and chin.

When he came downstairs, he found the other inmates of the house ready, and waiting for him. He thrust them forth and locked the door.

On the way to the New Hall they caught up and passed small parties of serious people, by twos and threes, walking silently and solemnly to the place of meeting.

From the lower part of the town pealed the brass band at the circus, and the flaring lights about the booth could be seen, even the black masses of people distinguished, who were crowding to the show.

"Look there, at the many," said Jabez Grice, sternly; "see here the few! I feel like Moses on the mount when he saw the people dancing and feasting. He broke all the commandments, he was in such anger. I could do the same."

Standing on the steps of the New Hall, and looking on the plain, the booths, the crowd, Jabez hastily, and with a jerk, opened his umbrella, shut it again, and opened it once more.

"I would," said he, "I would they was all swallowed up alive, like Korah and his company, them and their tents and their wives and their children. It'd be a lesson to some."

Then he turned and entered the hall and pushed his way to the platform, regardless of his son and sister, whom he left to settle where they pleased. The hall was very new, very white, and very glaring with the gas turned on full. It was but half filled, and the prospect of its filling was scanty. Already the hour for opening had struck, and those on the platform waited, hoping that more would arrive to replenish the body of the hall. Those who had come set up their greatcoats, mantles and umbrellas on the vacant seats at their sides to disguise, as far as might be, the emptiness.

On the platform were assembled the notables of the serious world at Saltwich. The chair was to be taken by Mr Nottershaw, architect, surveyor and builder. He stood well with the serious; it was his interest to do so. He spoke at their meetings, he subscribed to their charities, he appeared in their chapels, he sat on their committees, and he designed and erected for them their public buildings. He had indeed sent his children to the circus, with strict injunctions to sit in the cheap places with the crowd lest they should be recognised. The ministers of seven denominations were here sinking their differences and mutual jealousies. Dr Tallow, large, flat-faced, with bushy whiskers and very glossy black coat, and very starched white tie, was fanning himself with a printed copy of one of his own sermons.

As Jabez Grice ascended the platform, applause broke out from every portion of the room. Only the dummies of umbrella and greatcoat did not join in the ovation.

Andrew found it was impossible for him to collect his thoughts and make them wheel round Dr Tallow like the constellations about the sun. They wandered whilst the chairman was introducing the doctor and apologising for the smallness of the audience, with lamentations over the vanity of the minds that preferred circus-riding to the elocutionary gymnastics of the illustrious doctor from Jericho.

Andrew's mind was absent in the Old Hall Field, though his body was present in the New Hall. His father might command the one, he was powerless to control the other. He found himself listening to hear if he could catch, where he sat, any strains of the brass band wafted in through an open window. He found himself thinking over the programme, and picturing the scenes in the circus after the coloured posters. Was the little Queen now making her entrance in the mother-o'-pearl shell? How radiant, how beautiful she would be! and he was not there! She would look round for him—would miss him. She would be offended at his absence—she would not come on the morrow to see the salt works.

With an effort Andrew screwed his attention to Dr Tallow's discourse, and found that his mind was poisoned against him by the words of Rab—prejudiced against him by his own disappointment! That was true which Rab had said. He knew all the anecdotes—or others so like them that they were undistinguishable in their common silliness. He knew the illustrations—they were pointless. He could not endure the frothy eloquence. The topic of the discourse was commonplace, the delivery commonplace, the voice commonplace; he had heard it all a thousand times before, and he could find no interest in what he heard now for the thousand and first time.

He pulled out of his pocket a nut—it was one of those that had been offered him by Queenie. He looked at it. He fell into dreams over it. He turned it about. He held it up to the light. He saw in it the dints of her sharp little teeth—it was as though a squirrel had been biting at it. He looked closely at the depressions—No doubt about it at all. Those dints were the dints of teeth—of her teeth. Not considering where he was, what was going on, who was speaking, or whence the speaker came, nor what was the subject of his address, Andrew put the nut into his mouth and cracked it.

Those near him started. The lecturer paused. Those on benches and chairs in front turned, and, with indignant frowns, stared Andrew in the face. The sensation could hardly have been greater had Andrew discharged a bomb.

"When that young gentleman has finished his nuts, perhaps I may be allowed to proceed," said the doctor, with withering sarcasm.

The chairman interfered.

"There is a time for all things," said he. "If the frivolous choose to crack nuts at such a moment as this, under the outpour of such words as we have heard, let him go out from us—he is not of us."

"Turn him out!" was shouted from the further side of the hall, by those who had not seen that the culprit was the son of the respected Jabez Grice. Only the dummies of umbrella and greatcoat did not join in the remonstrance.

Abashed, Andrew took his cap, crept to the door, and slipped forth into the open air. He had as much as promised his father that he would not go to the circus, but he was free to prowl round it.

After the pause caused by the unseemly disturbance, the preacher caught up the thread of his discourse again and proceeded to draw it to an end.

Then rose Mr Poles, the paperhanger, to propose a vote of thanks to the American Demosthenes, the Jericho Chrysostom, who had come among them to deepen their seriousness. Mr Poles was a prolix speaker; his discourse consisted in a series of elocutionary festoons, and when done, no one could very well say what it had all been about. His place was at once occupied by Jabez Grice, who started to his feet and looked about him, not with diffidence, like Mr Poles, nor tremblingly holding to a chair-back, but planted with his solid feet wide apart, firm, confident, like the Colossus of Rhodes, set to give light to the voyagers on the sea of life; he spoke, not with a thin, timid, quavering voice, like the paperhanger, but with one rich, resonant and firm. There was nothing apologetic in his manner, his tone, his attitude. He asked to be heard because he insisted on being heard, and because he knew that he would be heard, and heard with avidity.

"My serious friends," began Jabez, and he eased his arms in his sleeves as he started speaking, and spread his breast; "it is a proud moment to me to stand before you on this undenominational platform, and to second the vote of thanks proposed to the illustrious stranger—who is yet not a stranger, as his printed volumes are familiar to all the seriously-disposed. It may be said that this undenominational gathering is unprecedented. I ask—What is precedent? Why should we consider precedent? This is the point to which I will address myself, and I pray you, lend me your attention for two minutes. Precedents, my serious friends, are the rags and tatters in which past ignorance enveloped itself, and which it hands on to the imbecile and weaklings and unreasoning of the present day, that they may cloak themselves in the same, when unable to give an account in the face of the world for what they are asked to do, which they know they ought to do, and yet which they dare not do. Respect for precedent belongs to a condition of mind and to a state of society out of which we have happily grown. *We* are not men of yesterday. We are men of to-day!"

Here ensued a burst of applause.

"We are not concerned with the judgments of the past. Men may have been fools then. If they did, and if they ruled foolish things then, are we to do foolish things to-day?"

Cries of "No! no!"

"It is degradation—it is an absurdity for us men of the nineteenth century to be ruled, not by reason, not by conscience, but by precedence. Let each question that arises be judged on its own merits, and let not the right or wrong of the question be obscured by the haze of precedent. Drag it into the full blaze of light. Discuss it with unengaged minds, and judge it as Heaven gives intelligence!"

Cries of "Hear! hear!"

"In the year 1847—let me tell you—the legislature of this country considered the introduction of a measure for the abolition of appeal to precedent. And let me tell you, there came up from all parts of Great Britain a petition, signed by seven millions of rational men and women, praying for the abolition of appeal to precedent. With what result?"

The audience held its breath. The speaker looked round.

"With what result? That the petition was ordered to lie on the table. There were found, my friends, in the legislature and outside of it, men— creatures, I should rather term them, with their tails turned to the present age of light, and their nozzles turned to the past age of obscurity—who raised objections, as such creatures always will, to every salutary alteration. And the measure was defeated on the grounds—on the grounds that there was *no precedent for rejecting the appeal to precedent.*"

The speaker looked round with defiance, his mouth shut, his brows knit, his hands clenched.

"The English people had said their say—and were silenced. This was in the beginning of the nineteenth century. They sat down and were content. They would not sit down and be content now. Why not? Because they live further on in the nineteenth century than did those memorialists. Now, if they say their say, and are not heard, they shout their shout; and if their shout be not listened to, then they roar their roar; and then heard they are. Heard they must be, for heard they will to be."

Immense applause, in which only the dummies of umbrella and greatcoat did not join.

Then some one, far back in the hall, stood up, and said,—

"May I be allowed to ask some particulars relative to this very remarkable bill brought before the House, of which I had never heard? May I ask where further particulars may be found?"

Jabez Grice was ready at once with an answer.

"I know," said he, in his loud and resonant tones,

"both whence this interruption proceeds, and what is its object. That gentleman who has put a question to me has deliberately distorted my words—I did not say, I purposely did *not* say, that this motion was debated in the House. I said that it was considered by the Ministry of the day. I have yet to learn that the deliberations of the Cabinet are recorded in the statutes at large, and the thoughts of the Ministry find their place in the 'Transactions of Parliament.' Let me advise that person who has interrupted with his frivolous question, in future to use his ears, and not allow his imagination play; let me advise him to cultivate accuracy. I am not bound to meet captious questions. This is not the place in which to dissipate crass ignorance. But enough of this topic, and of this gentleman. I wipe him out of my memory. I return to the point from which I was drawn away."

"Father!" said Andrew. He was below the platform and had laid hold of his father's foot. "Pray, do come. You are greatly wanted. You are wanted immediately."

"What is it?" asked Grice impatiently.

"There has been a terrible accident. A subsidence at the circus."

"I said it—as I came in at the door I said it," shouted Grice with triumph in his face—in his tone. "I turned on the door-step of this hall and denounced the revellers, and said—'Let the earth open her mouth and let them go down quick into the abyss.'"

"Father, I beseech you, come! Your brother—Santi—"

"Well?"

Is dying, and crying out for you."

CHAPTER IX.

BROTHER OR NO BROTHER?

"You need not have shouted out that he was my brother," said Jabez, as he walked from the New Hall to Old Hall Field with his son at his side.

"Father, I did not shout. I thought that I whispered."

"Well, you whispered loud enough for all on the platform to hear, and interrupted me in the middle of my speech—and a very important speech it was."

"What was I to say? There has been a terrible affair. A subsidence where the circus was."

"That was right enough. I don't object to the subsidence, nor to your telling me of it."

"Signor Santi is frightfully injured, and is asking for you as his brother."

"Couldn't you have said he was asking for me, and have stayed there, instead of blurting out what followed, instead of proclaiming what is a lie and an insult."

"I knew nothing of that. I never supposed you would take the matter so, father. The dying man said he had no one in the world to ask for but you, his brother."

"He is not my brother—never was. My father married again after my mother's death, and took a young widow with her son by her first husband. That was Joe Sant. How can he be my brother when we don't share a drop of blood? All we ever did share were bed and bread and butter. He is no relation of mine. I have nothing to do with him. He took his road; I took mine—and his was the broad and evil way."

"But you are going to see him, father?"

"Of course, I am. I'll see him. I do what is right."

"Hammer" Grice said no more, but strode along. At every step he took, he planted his foot on the earth as though he were taking possession of the soil for ever.

After he had gone forward some way in silence, he halted and said,—

"How has it come about? A subsidence?"

"Yes, father; I suppose the earth wouldn't bear the extra weight and the trampling. The Old Field has been held to be insecure for some time. But I suppose the poor fellows thought it would hold up as long as they needed it. Now the deepest point is not under the circus, it is between it and the flash, but the ground has given way, cracked, sunk, and the earth has begun to run, and as it ran, down came the structure, boards and canvas and all."

"Many killed?"

"I do not know, father. I was at the meeting as you know. When I went out, I ran down to the Old Field because I learned that something had happened there, and I could hear the screams and the general uproar from the steps of the Town Hall. I know very little more than what I was told when I asked—and then I heard that the manager had been extricated from under the tent, and that he was terribly cut about and crushed. I don't know whether the pole fell across him, or whether he was trodden on by the horses. He has been badly burned also, for there was fire that somehow broke out. Fellows were saying he had been taken to his van, and they had drawn that away out of danger of sinking, and they had sent for a doctor. They told me he was calling for you. He had no one in the world to look to but you, he said, and none to provide for but his daughter."

"He has a daughter?"

"Yes; the Queen of Love."

"The Queen of Love! He is surely not going to saddle me with her! The Queen of Love in my serious family! A hussy with short skirts in Alma Terrace!"

He remained stationary, brooding over the prospect.

"That would be a fine confusion! The Queen of Love—with her heathenish ways, her skipping ropes and butterfly habits, and all the pomps—in No. 4. Deliver us!"

He strode on.

Had he any idea of the sudden flutter of hope that stirred, the flash, the blaze, of an opening world of light and beauty and love, that broke on the imagination of the youth at his side as he said these words? None whatever—not an inkling. Jabez Grice had no thought of Andrew at all. He was considering the discomfort, the contrarieties to himself, the scandals that might ensue in his house, were this discordant element to be introduced into his serious family.

"Perhaps Joe Sant is not so bad after all," said he, drawing a long breath. "He'll move on, and take his precious set of belongings with him. The sooner the better."

On reaching Old Hall Field, it was found to present a scene of confusion from which it had not begun to recover. In the nightlight, the circus presented the appearance of a stranded and wrecked hull. Nor was it free from the attacks of wreckers. For it had occurred to a good many of the idle and unscrupulous that there were boards in the wreck which could be converted into poultry-houses with very little labour; that there was red repp and baize enough to make petticoats for whole families, and that there was rope that would come in handy as lines on which to hang clothes after washing day. One or two men were cutting slices out of the canvas, wherewith to make themselves jackets and trousers.

The police were there, but the number stationed at Saltwich was small, and they were directing search parties among the ruins to save lives, rather than spending their energies in the protection of property. The night was dark; they could not follow the proceedings of the depredators, though they might suspect that depredations were being carried on. Their first duties were towards such as were still entangled in the canvas, or were lying injured among the fallen woodwork. Apparently very few persons had been seriously hurt. Some were bruised; here and there it was reported that bones had been broken. No one was missing—umbrellas, reticules, baskets of refreshments lay about under the boards, and these were the principal losses. Some children were astray, but their violent screams led to attention being directed to them, and, as they were able to give an account of themselves, to their speedy restoration to their homes.

The clown and Signora Muslina were the principal

persons who seemed to be in grave distress. They could nowhere find the second performing dog, Tweedledee. They ran about, followed or preceded by Tweedledum. The dog was whining, the signora remonstrating in shrill, harsh tones; the clown, her husband, screaming, because Tweedledee did not respond to their calls, and could not be seen or heard of on any side. The signora—her proper name was Mrs Nelson, Bell Nelson, in the troupe—had thrown a rug round her bare shoulders, but her spidery and somewhat exposed legs, encased in white stockings, under scanty muslin skirts, were everywhere distinguishable, running, jumping, climbing after Tweedledee; and the heart of the poor signora was sore under the spangles that overlay it, and she had screamed herself hoarse in her distress for the loss of the dear dog.

The workmen in white jackets belonging to the show, the trapezists, and one of the performers on horseback, the Modern Proteus, the man who balanced balls and waved flags, lent ready help; so did some of the grooms from the stables, cheerful and obliging. Boys and men went about with lanterns. It was as though a swarm of fireflies had settled down on the Old Hall Field. Some had brought together chips, broken pieces of deal and lumps of coal, and had made a fire, that threw light on the ruined circus and the crowd, wavering and interweaving in incessant change around it.

Andrew led his father in the direction of the gilded and painted van in which lay the injured man. About it were collected the horses, the bison, the ostriches that had been brought away from the endangered tract of land. The animals could not understand the condition of affairs. They made strange noises. The ostriches brayed like donkeys, the horses plunged and kicked out. The routine of their lives was broken in on, and they had lost their sense of obedience. The men who usually attended to them were those in white jackets, and they were engaged elsewhere. Their places had been taken by volunteers from various stables, but these did not understand circus beasts, or the beasts did not understand being handled by strangers.

Grice entered the van without a word to anyone. The van was divided interiorly into compartments. The first entered was the parlour; it had benches at the sides, stuffed and covered with leather. The windows were hung with pretty curtains. In the middle was a stove, and against one of the sides, under a casement, was fastened a desk, at which the director did all his accounts and correspondence.

Through a door opposite the entrance, access was obtained to the bedroom. There lay Santi, on his narrow pallet, as complete a wreck as his show. He had been trampled on by the cream-coloured horses,

BROTHER OR NO BROTHER? 99

crushed by the falling pole, and burned by the overset lamps. A surgeon had been summoned, and he had stripped off the man's frock coat and waistcoat, and had examined him. One of the acrobats was kneeling at the sufferer's head and holding it on his arm. He was dressed as a wild Indian, painted brown with red lips, and wore moccasins on his legs and a plumed head-dress.

The surgeon stood up and shook his head.

The Indian's brown face turned to him, watching intently.

"Done for, manager, done for," said the fellow in tones of deep and tender feeling. "You must try and bear it as a man, old fellow. We must all come to it some day. Shall I put your head a little more on one side? Are you easy? Or shall I stay you up in my arms, boss? You are as feeble and helpless as when you took me up."

"Thank you, Seth, it will do."

"Oh, boss, I wish it was I, crumpled up and done for, and not you. But, old boss, I'm afraid I wouldn't be as ready to go as are you. Boss, when you come to the place where we must all appear, you can hold up your poor achin' head and tell the story o' that there baby boy, Seth—how you took and keared for the horphan, and fed and clothed him, free, gratis, when he could be nort but an expense; and how you taught him to know right from wrong. And if it please the pigs that I come to where you be going—Lord, it'll be all your doin'! For what would I ha' been but for you!"

Then the Red Indian began to sob, and the tears to stream down his painted cheeks.

"I've never had none but you, boss, and little Queenie to kear about in the world. Oh, dear! oh, dear! and what is to become of her?"

"Don't take on, Seth; you've been a good boy."

"I do take on, boss! I can't help it. And you're going to leave us and the hostriches and the 'osses, and that there darned idjot of a buffalo, as won't mind none of us, but your word only. But there, we won't think o' that. Put your hands together. You can't? That there old arm be broke, is it? Well, put that right hand up from off your heart, boss dear, and I'll put my left from under your neck against it, and we'll say the prayer together—as you taught me when I was a little creetur."

Then the Indian lifted the dying man against his breast, and put his palm against that of the other, and with sobs and broken voice repeated,—

"Meek and mild—look on me—a little child—pity my simplicity"—he wiped his face. "It don't suit altogether; 'tisn't that I meant. But it comes to my mind first, and yet, old man, you're now weak as a babe, just as I was when you took me up, and keared for me, and taught me them words; and if it ain't quite what it ort to be, well, I daresay it will be overlooked."

"I think I can do better for the poor fellow than that," said Jabez Grice, stepping forward. "You don't seem to know what you're about. How can you? Grapes don't come of thorns and figs of thistles."

"My brother Jabez!" exclaimed the dying man—and held out the one hand he could command.

"I am sorry to see you like this, Joe," said Grice. He took his hand, then, turning to all who were present, said,—"He is not really my brother. We are in no ways related."

The dying manager looked steadily into the face of Jabez.

"You were always a serious boy," he said; "I suppose you're serious still."

"Certainly."

"Then I'm sure I can trust you. You were a good boy."

"What is right—that I do—of course. I couldn't do other," answered Grice.

"I want to speak alone with you."

The manager was in pain. It was with an effort that he gathered his thoughts; with an effort and manifest suffering that he spoke. His eyes were sunken. They seemed more sunken than they really were, owing to the shadow cast by the strong light of the lamp hanging from the ceiling of the cabin.

"Must I go, boss?" asked the Red Indian, from whose cheeks much of the paint had come away.

Santi nodded—then with his hand caught his arm, and said,—

"Her—my little Queenie. I haven't seen her! Tell me she is not hurt—tell me where she is. I want to say good-bye to Queenie—Seth, go and find her. Tell her—her father— Bring her to me!"

His head sank back on the pillow. He breathed with pain. His ribs were crushed on the lungs.

"I am sorry to say I can be of no more use," observed the surgeon, taking his hat; "if I could, I would cheerfully stay, but as—"

He left the room with the sentence unfinished.

Grice waved a sign to his son to leave, and Andrew went outside.

When left alone with the manager, Jabez said,—

"I was afraid it would come to this. You never took my warnings when we were young together. I have gone my way—you have gone yours—and now you are struck down in your iniquities."

"Iniquities—what iniquities?" asked Santi, faintly.

"Skipping-ropes and butterflies, and muslin and fleshings, and all the pomps," said Grice, solemnly.

"I don't know," the dying man gasped. "I've tried to be true and just in all my dealings. If I haven't— I've been sorry. I mayn't have been all I ought to have been, and I don't deny it—I don't deny it. I feel it here." He lightly touched his heart—he was breathing painfully. "There was that pictur of a boa-constrictor swallering of a man. I wouldn't have it up—outside the show. I hadn't a boa. Bell Nelson offered to lend me her fur one—and sew it up in canvas and paint it. But I wouldn't—'twasn't true." He remained silent awhile, breathing with labouring chest. "And I've tried to be just. If I haven't, by mistake it has been—not by intent. That's how I've made so much money."

"Money!" repeated Grice in astonishment.

"Yes—horses, and skipping-ropes and hoops, and muslin and all that—it has been my profession. The profession ain't amiss. I've made money. And I've always invested my savings every year—for Queenie. Stay—I can't speak." He seemed to lapse into unconsciousness, but rallied. "You were awfully strict and serious as a boy," said the manager, his great eyes turning searchingly on Grice. "Get a pen and paper from my desk. It's—in 'tother place. I can't trust Nelson—he drinks. Seth White is too young—I've no one else but you. I must trust you —for Queenie — little Queenie!" He turned his head. "I want to see her—to kiss her. Bring my Queenie here. I've worked, and slaved, and put by for her. Bring Queenie. There's a good deal of money."

Grice went into the outer compartment, and returned with paper and pen and ink.

"There is no time to be lost," he said. "Money, you said. A good deal of it. I shouldn't have thought it, brother Joe. My dear brother Joe."

CHAPTER X.

AN ORPHAN.

QUEENIE sat in the high-backed chair by the fire in the cottage of the Rainbows. The walls of the chamber were painted sky-blue, and were of appalling brilliancy—the colour affected, possibly, as some contrast to the red-brick of the exterior. There stood a dresser against the wall, on which were ranged plates, jugs and bowls of Bristol lustre-ware that shone like burnished copper—or as the hair of the little maiden who leaned back in the chair.

She was in her white gauze dress, strewn with spangles. At every breath a flash, as of summer lightning, shot over her bosom, in the reflections of the great fire, and an incessant quiver of light was in her thistle-down skirts, produced by the slightest movement of her limbs.

She was recovered from her insensibility, but much shaken, and one ankle was sprained. Her arms were bare; one was raised, and the hand thrust behind her head. The little feet were crossed in their white satin shoes, and rested on a hassock.

Mrs Rainbow had put the kettle on the fire to boil, so as to make Queenie a cup of tea, after which she was to be put to bed. Sheets and blankets were tossed across chair-backs to air, and Rab's mother was on her knees with a pail, scrubbing the floor.

"Mother!" said Rab, in a tone of impatience, "why do you set to wash the floor now? Can't it wait till to-morrow?"

"No, it can't," answered the woman, standing up. She was a tall, handsome woman, very untidy in her person, and dressed incongruously, with an old hat on her head that had belonged to her deceased husband, and a tattered jacket of Rab's over her back. "No, it can't," said she. "If you choose to bring dirt in on your boots, I ain't going to let it remain ten minutes. Lor! the work you do bring on me. And never a thought for your old mother."

Mrs Rainbow was a person of immense energy; she worked, she verily slaved from morning till night; and yet was neither tidy herself, nor had her house neat. How, with all the work she did, so little result was visible—that was a marvel to her son. She did a little bartering with vegetables on a hand-cart she ran along herself; she had a little shop, that is to say, sold lollipops, peppermints, oranges and ginger-beer; she kept geese on the common, and fowls in the back-yard. She picked up pennies by this means, and professed that, but for herself, the house never could have been kept going.

"I'll clean up whenever dirt comes in," said Mrs Rainbow. "The kettle won't boil all at once, nor the blankets get aired of a jiffy."

Rab was on one knee before the fire, toasting bread, but his eyes were on Queenie. The girl's right hand was resting on her lap. Presently her cheek puckered with a smile, and, raising her finger, she pointed at Rab's cap.

He at once removed his headgear, put down the toast, and, unpinning the bruised and withered yellow rose, said,—

"You gave me this."

He put his hand into his breast-pocket, and drew forth a much-used letter-case, in which were flies for fishing, and scraps of newspaper relative to races, and, folding the rose in a piece of clean paper, he threw out all the racing notes and flies, placed the rose within, and then put the case into his pocket again.

"There!" said he. "I shall not part with this flower till my dying day. Remember that, little Queen of Love. It is the first flower ever given me, and you gave it me when I had been very bold and rude, and by it showed you had forgiven me. When I'm dead, little Queen, then—if I have not taken the yaller leaves underground with me—do me a kindness and strew 'em on my grave."

"I'll find you a better rose."

"I want none other. This will do for me. I am sorry I was rude, but Andrew angered me."

"Who is Andrew?"

"Oh, he is a good boy—an uncommon good boy; and I," Rab shrugged his shoulders, "I'm a shocking bad un."

"Ah, never was a truer word spoken!" exclaimed Mrs Rainbow, rising from her slops. "A precious life you have led your old mother, what with your idleness, and poachings, and drinkings and skylarkings."

"Do you drink?" asked Queenie.

"Sometimes—always on washing days, and when mother's tongue is loose at the joints."

"I'll tell you what it is," said Mrs Rainbow. "There will be no toast done at this rate—staring into a gal's face, instead of minding the bread before the fire."

Rab hastened to resume his operation of toasting.

"I am sorry you drink," said the girl.

"So am I," answered Rab. "But I can't help it."

"That's what our clown says. He'd be a first-rate clown and a good fellow, but he can't keep from the public-house. Father cautioned him over and over— he came fresh to the performances, and was not in the least funny then. He cried. So father has had to lock him up in an old monkey cage he bought of a menagerie man, who broke because his monkeys all got the influenza. Father locks him up directly we get into a town, and keeps him there till it is time to get ready for the performance. And Bell Nelson, she walks up and down with a switch and has the key. She does not let him out till he is summoned to paint and dress."

"A very good thing too," said Mrs Rainbow. "I'll treat you the same, Rab; I'll shut you up in the goose-pen—and serve you right."

"Does the clown submit?" asked the young man.

"He must—and he knows it's for his good. And Bell, she walks up and down and puts her nose between the bars, and gives him her mind. He can't break out as before. It must be after a performance. Father can't keep him all day and all night in the monkey cage—"

"Now, then! Now, then!" shouted Mrs Rainbow. "I don't call that toast. You've got the bread against the bars. I'd like to make a zebra of you as you've been treating that slice."

"Where is my father?" asked Queenie. "I want to see him. Is he safe?"

"I brought you away," said Rab. "I really know nothin' more than that you are here."

"I remember the creamies turned restive, and they made a start."

"Yes—the earth cracked before them."

"Let me manage toasting the bread. Do, pray, go and ask after my dear father!" said the girl.

"Listen to the voice of nat'ral affection," said Mrs Rainbow, standing up with a scrubbing brush in one hand and a bar of soap in the other. "Hear her hollering for her father. It's a thousand years since I've heard my son call after his mammy like that, and I reckon it'll be a thousand years more before he comes round to know his duty to his mother." She rubbed her eyes with the soap, then, as that made them sting, with the scrubbing brush. "As for Rab, if I but shows the end of my tongue, off he goes like a cricket before the light—to the public-house."

A tap at the door, and when the woman opened, she sprang back with an exclamation of terror. A Red Indian, hung with scalps, was in the doorway; he was dazzled by the light, and asked somewhat hesitatingly.—

"Is the little Queen here?"

"It's Seth! It's Seth!" exclaimed the girl, starting out of her chair, and then, finding her foot give way under, sinking back into it again.

"Queenie! Do I hear you?" said the Red Indian. "I'm terribly grieved; you must come at once."

"Oh, Seth, Seth, what is the matter?"

"I am sorry to say—your father is bad!"

The girl uttered a piercing cry, and tried to limp to the door.

"You cannot walk," said Rab. "I carried you before; I will carry you agin. Mother, a shawl."

The young man carefully, tenderly, folded a great red wrap round the girl, so as to completely cover her, with the exception of her golden hair, which flowed out and over the shawl, and hung on Rab's shoulder like tresses of laburnum on a wall. He bore her lightly along, and the painted Indian stepped at his side.

"There's a lot of our chaps about the wan as wants to see the boss"—he looked significantly towards the bundle. "I mean, they've heard the signor ain't quite up to tune, you know, and they're all dying to shake his hand and say a word. But there's a fellow in the wan, as says he's the signor's brother, won't let 'em in, not one of them. They take on dreadful about it."

"Are all your company safe?"

"Yes; I guess all but Tweedledee."

"Who's Tweedledee?"

"It's one of the performin' dawgs. There's a pair of them; they belong to the Nelsons, that is, to the clown and to her—the lady as goes through the fiery hoop, you know. The master pays so much a week for their services, and they're uncommon clever dawgs. But Tweedledee's amissin', so the Nelsons are in a pretty stew."

They had not far to go.

"Some chap said he'd seen the little Queen carried into one of them cottages," said the Red Indian; "and he told me 'twas that of the Rainbows. *He*—you know who I mean—he's been axing for her. I guess that brother who is there won't deny her admittance."

"I'll force open the door if he does," said Rab.

They had reached the van. About the steps stood the members of the company. Some of those in fleshings had succeeded in getting coats to throw over them, as the night was raw. A curious mixture of persons was congregated before the van, in which a man was dying. Every face, as far as could be distinguished by a flaming light, showed signs of distress through the paint that obscured the natural features. A good deal of murmuring, and many a lamentation, broke from the kindly, affectionate hearts of these vagabonds.

"He was a master—a good un," said one of the acrobats. "He never swore at a chap on the trapeze till he lost his nerve, as I've knowed some do."

"Ay! he was a good chap!" said another. "Look what he done for that boy Seth."

"And he paid regular, down on the nail," said a third.

The clown was stealing away on tiptoe, in the shadow of the van; his wife was aware of the manœuvre, and went after him, caught him by the roll on one of his shoulders, and dragged him back.

"For shame, Jim! for shame! you unnat'ral beast! when the dear master's dying! I know what you're after; you ha'n't got no money, but you think you can find chaps as will stand treat."

"I was going to have another look for Tweedledee," said the clown.

"No, you wasn't, you was after liquor. I won't have it! It's fortunate the monkey cage is safe. I've seed it! That's not swallered up, and I've got the key!"

"Oh, Bell, dearest Bell, darling, I'm never put in that after a performance."

"I'll put you in, and keep you in, if you demean yourself, and at such a time as this!"

Rab, with Seth at his side, pushed up the steps. Rab did not stay to knock—he opened the door. At once Jabez Grice started to intercept him, but Rab looked him straight in the face, and said,—

"Here is his daughter."

Grice drew aside, and allowed Rab, carrying the girl, to enter the inner room, followed by the Red Indian. Then, at once, the rest of the company pressed in. It was too late to repel them. One of the acrobats had planted himself against the door, so that Grice could not shut it. He hesitated, saw that it was not possible for him now to drive out the crowd, and they came thick on his heels, in all their motley, through the front compartment into the bed-chamber, and there spread out in silence, with folded arms and bowed heads. In the midst, by the bed, knelt Rab; he unfurled the red shawl, and let the girl, in her spangles and muslin, flash and twinkle in the eyes of her dying father.

"Bear up, child, bear up," he whispered.

The little Queen seemed turned to marble. She could not speak. She could hardly breathe. She could not move. It was all too terrible, too crushing for the childish heart. With great open, dark eyes, full of despair, she looked on her father's drawn face, altered by pain, haggard as she had never conceived his face could become. She put her hands over her eyes to shut out the sight, then withdrew them again.

Then she caught his one hand extended to her from the bed, and squeezed it frantically to her glittering bosom.

The eyes of the dying man looked round the tiny, crowded compartment of the van, and sought Grice. Then he withdrew his hand from his daughter, pointed to Jabez, and said,—

"Listen all! I trust her to a good man, a good man. You will go to him, Queenie!"

He closed his eyes and laid his hand on his bosom.

"What is it?" asked Seth, stooping over the dying man.

"Meek and mild,
Look upon a little child!"

The words, broken, faint, tremulous, were the last

the manager, Signor Santi, uttered. To whom did they apply? To himself rendered helpless as a babe, or to his daughter left an orphan?

Then Grice drew between the bed, and the staring, frightened, stupefied Queenie, and said to Rab,—

"Take her away—it is over."

Suddenly a wave of gold poured over the poacher's face, dazzling, smothering him. The child had turned, thrown her arms round his neck with a bitter cry, and burst into convulsive sobs.

CHAPTER XI.

ADA BUTTON.

JABEZ GRICE was not the man to yield in difficulties, least of all in such as were of a sentimental nature. When he made up his mind to a course, he neither swerved from it himself, nor endured that any impediments be put in his way by others.

Grice was speedily made aware that the troupe had set their minds on making of the funeral of their manager a grand demonstration. They would attend in a body, and ride the circus horses. Some qualms came over them relative to the propriety of introducing the buffalo and the ostriches in the procession, none whatever as to the suitability of the creamies and a piebald pony. The late director's Arab was to walk, or rather limp, behind his coffin, with the boots reversed slung over the saddle.

Grice, with decision, put a stop to their scheme. He, and he alone, was responsible for the funeral arrangements. The interment was to take place with the utmost quiet and privacy. None were to attend save those related to the deceased. He would not even inform the troupe of the day when the funeral was to take place.

To prevent, as far as might be, any unauthorised accession to the ranks of mourners, Grice summoned the members of the company before him in the late manager's van, opened his books and paid every man and woman what arrears were claimed, and a month in advance, and requested them to make themselves as scarce as possible in Saltwich. The clown put in a demand for compensation for the loss of Tweedledee, but it was so extortionate that Grice refused to listen to it, and the clown was forced to depart, guarded by his wife, with their united salaries alone.

Jabez was a man of cool head, promptitude and practical knowledge. He resolved to make the best sale he could effect of the horses, vans and properties of the circus. He proposed advertising the whole in London and Manchester, and if no offer came within a fortnight, to dispose of the various lots, piecemeal, by auction, not at Saltwich, but at Crewe. If any of the old company were prepared with a bid they were welcome to remove the entire concern, only Grice would accept no promises to pay. Let it be clearly understood, he parted with the circus, and all belonging to it, cash down. Some of the troupe put their heads together and considered whether it were possible to put their pockets together as well. But it proved that though they could furnish any amount of undertaking to pay, they were not able, singly or conjointly, to find the requisite sum for buying the stock. Money-lenders were shy of advancing money to a rambling band whose whereabouts was not always ascertainable.

The troupe again put their heads together. They felt it a duty to attend their old master to the grave. But there were difficulties in the way of their performing this duty beside those presented by the action of Grice. To attend a funeral necessitated mourning. Now, almost every colour was represented in the private wardrobes of the company but black. The principal acrobat affected blue trousers; the main performer on horseback, when in private, wore a very light, snuff-coloured suit and a Stuart plaid waistcoat. Bell Nelson's best gown was of copperas green. If they were all to go into mourning, a great hole would be made in the small available sum they had to maintain them till they could be re-engaged. Then, again, time was of almost as great importance as money. They must at once seek new situations, and, considering the competition in this, as in every trade, it was possible that those slow in offering themselves might be left out in the cold altogether. The only men really unconcerned about their future were the two carpenters and a fellow who had attended to the horses. These knew that they would find ready employ anywhere; and, in fact, the latter was at once engaged to one of the stud stables on the edge of Delamere Forest.

As yet, Queenie remained in the cottage of the Rainbows. Grice had been unable to receive her into his house, owing to lack of accommodation or of furniture, but he made provision for her removal immediately after the funeral.

The troupe had pretty well dispersed before that took place. But Seth White, who had personated a Red Indian, remained. No consideration would induce him to leave till after the burial of the man who had taken care of him when a helpless infant.

The day on which Joe Sant, or Signor Santi as he was professionally called, was taken to his grave was not cheerful. The clouds hung low and were unoutlined, forming one dense, dull canopy of grey, like dirty wadding. Trees, fields, herbs had lost brilliancy of colour. The roads were deep in red mud. There were no showers, nor continuous rain, but large warm drops fell at intervals. Those who carried umbrellas never knew quite whether to unfurl them or not. The hedges were dripping, the birds flew low; a crow occasionally called, but no song-birds sang. The cattle stood moping in the fields without spirit to gambol, without appetite to browse.

The air was warm, and dense with minute gnats, and wherever there was garbage, swarms of long-legged flies wavered over the engaging morsels. The gnats were everywhere. They got into the hair, into the ears; they stung the temples and the wrists, they produced a sense of general irritation.

The hearse that contained the body of Joe Sant, followed by one mourning coach, was in the road to Scatterley Church, distant two miles, and slowly progressed between hedges rank with docks, and ditches choked with sting-nettles. The same vehicle and the same driver that had conveyed the deputation to Mr Button, to remonstrate with him on the concession, to the mountebanks, of the New Hall Field, were now engaged to transport the mourners to Scatterley. For the occasion, the driver had donned his weeper and drawn his mouth down at the corners.

Jabez Grice, Beulah his sister, Queenie and Andrew, occupied the interior of the coach. Grice and his sister sat in the back part and held white pocket-handkerchiefs in their hands. Grice had a black suit always ready for such occasions, and Beulah had managed to contrive a bonnet and gown out of pre-existing materials; but Andrew had to be submitted to a tailor, and a dressmaker had been sent to the Rainbows' cottage with instructions to provide all that was necessary for the girl. Behind the carriage, unobserved by Grice and his sister, walked Rab Rainbow and Seth White. They had joined the funeral procession, uninvited and unnoticed, and were dressed up in such scraps of black as they had been able to scrape together. Queenie, weeping, half-blinded with tears, raised her heavy eyes, and looking at intervals through the window at her side, saw the figure of Rab lurching along in the rear, his trousers turned halfway up his calves, splashing through the mud, and bespattered by the carriage wheels in front. Horses are slower in their walk than men, and the two who were behind had some difficulty in accommodating their pace to the rate at which hearse and coach progressed. They could have walked the distance in half the time.

Rab's eyes were never off the carriage window, through which he could see the black figure of Queenie with her golden hair, which even the dulness of the day could not deaden; he could see how pale she was, how red were her eyes, and his whole frame quivered when he observed how she went into a convulsion of weeping behind the white kerchief that veiled her eyes.

He said nothing to his fellow-mourner all the way, and that way seemed interminable. They passed a red brick barn, with yellow lichen-spotted tiles on the roof, and a boulder of drift granite lying against the wall, with the water from the roof, that should have run in a shoot, as it settled or condensed, dripping over the stone.

As the carriage passed the barn, the bell of Scatterley Church was heard tolling.

About Saltwich there were no trees; the fumes from the brine-boiling works blighted, killed vegetation. But the vapours were comparatively inocuous at a distance of a couple of miles, and there were flourishing plantations of fir, some twelve to twenty feet high, about the parsonage.

Here the road made a rapid sweep, and in this sweep the hearse drew up at the churchyard gates. The driver descended from the coach and placed his hand on the door, to prevent those inside from opening, till the coffin had been removed from the hearse, the pall thrown over it, and the bearers were ranged in order.

Presently a nod from the undertaker gave the signal, and the driver raised his hat with one hand, and with the other opened the coach door and let down the steps.

Grice and Andrew descended first, then his sister and Queenie.

Now for the first time did Jabez observe the followers. He looked at them deliberately from head to foot, with an air of surprise, as though resenting their presence as an impertinent intrusion. Seth instinctively and apologetically touched his cap.

Rab coloured, bent and turned down his trousers over his muddy boots.

The church bell had stopped. In the graveyard path could be seen the parson in surplice, book in hand, waiting to read the opening sentences. At that moment round the curve of the road in front dashed a pony carriage driven by a young lady in colours. The road was not broad. The coffin and the hearse perhaps occupied an undue portion of it, so as greatly to reduce that in which a carriage could pass.

In the steamy, heavy air, the sound of the bell had been lost. The girl was quite unprepared to encounter a funeral train. The suddenness of the meeting prevented her from using her judgment. Instead of at once backing as she ought to have done, though it would have been difficult, she whipped the cob so as to dash past. There was nothing intentional in this exhibition of disrespect. She was confused, and endeavoured to extricate herself from an awkward position in the way that seemed readiest.

But the horse would not proceed; he started back, and in so doing threw her on to the front seat. The sombreness of the vehicles, the black of the mourners, the flapping of the sable velvet pall, edged with white—perhaps the savour of death—had frightened the cob, and it was now almost beyond the girl's control. She gathered herself up on her knees on the front seat of the open trap, grasped the reins short and lashed savagely at the horse.

"Go on, you brute, go on! you shall!" she said.

The bearers drew aside, they were afraid the cob would strike them with his hoofs; moreover, by so doing only, could room be made for the light carriage to pass. The horse would not obey. Again the girl raised her arm and beat him, again, and yet again. Her face was white, her thin lips set. There was no token of fear in her countenance, but it was lined with marks of resolution. What she had made up her mind that the horse should do, that she would make the horse do.

The two men, Rab and Seth, behind the mourning coach, could ill see what was taking place ahead of them, owing to the bend in the road, and they had not ventured to follow close on the authorised mourners.

One of the bearers stepping forward said,—

"Miss! shall I lead him past?"

"No thanks, I'll make him obey."

Again she thrashed the cob.

"Back him, miss," shouted the undertaker.

"He shall go on," said the girl; and then, finding that the beast would not proceed, in the blindness of one in anger, she struck at the coffin with her whip, and said,—"Take that away. It frightens him!"

In a moment Queenie, limping, but forgetful that

she was lame in her boiling indignation at the insult, ran to the little low carriage, snatched the whip out of the young lady's hands, broke it over her knee, and threw the pieces in her face, saying,—

"May you never have a coffin, never enjoy Christian burial—you hard heart!"

Rab and Seth had now thrust themselves forward and seized the bit. They led the foaming, trembling, panting beast past; and the girl who had been driving, with white, unmoved, or well-controlled face, resumed her place in the back seat, and said no word of apology or excuse.

"That is Ada Button," said Jabez, aside, to Beulah.

CHAPTER XII.

RAB'S RIGHT.

WHEN the funeral was over, Queenie returned to the cottage in Heathendom.

The quickly-kindled wrath had as quickly expired. The stroke of the horsewhip across her father's coffin had cut her quivering heart, and, in a spasm of anguish and rage, she had flown to resent it, had snatched the whip from this young lady, broken it and flung it in her face. On her way back in the coach to Saltwich, if her mind reverted at all from her great loss and sense of desolation to the incident at the churchyard gates, it was with a pang of self-reproach. A generous, frank nature, such as hers, would not admit the idea that the act which had roused her anger could have been one of intentional insult, or would not admit it for more than the flash of an instant. There was no malice in the stroke; it was dealt accidentally in the struggle with the horse. In the moment of explosion of anger, her eyes suffused with tears and dazzled by passion, she had not taken note of the girl in the carriage. She would hardly recognise her again.

During the return journey, which was performed at a slow trot, Grice and Beulah made no allusion to the incident.

Queenie was driven on to Heathendom, where she was to pack up her few clothes, and such trifles as she could call her own. The coach was to wait for her and bring her uphill to Alma Terrace. Her sprained ankle was not sufficiently restored to allow of her making the journey on foot. Mrs Rainbow had been kind to Queenie after her fashion—talking incessantly, glorying in her grievances against her son, her neighbours, her customers. She was a restless woman, and, not content with being in a perpetual fidget herself, she would allow no one in the house to be quiet.

Queenie was not sorry to leave. She felt that she could not have endured that woman many weeks. But she was not prepossessed in favour of Jabez Grice, who frightened her with his peremptory manner; nor of Beulah, in whom there was little to attract if nothing to repel.

The lonely girl hastily collected her goods and tied them up in a bundle, said farewell to Mrs Rainbow, promised to visit her again, and saw, with surprise, that this rough, restless woman was crying at her departure.

"My word! Whatever will Rab say at your going? Rab had made up his mind you would stay here. Rab will be angry with me for letting you go; and yet it is just as well. Rab is not a fellow to be trusted, and you are not a sort that would do for my boy to be with. I'll tell you the kind of woman he must find— one like that Mrs Nelson, who will lock him up if he misconducts himself. I am sorry you are going for my sake, glad for yours. You are going to tremendously respectable people, and we're not that—that's the fact. There's no denying it. Rab won't let us be. I tew from morning till night; but what can a woman do against a man? He upsets in one minute what it has taken me a day to order. I'm glad you are going. This ain't a fit place for a decent girl. You haven't seen Rab drunk yet. Wait till then, and you will pity me the life I lead. Yet—he is my own child, and I can't help myself. I suppose I must go on till he knocks my brains out with the poker. That's what it will come to some day."

The change to the house of the Grices was a change in every way. All things there were in order, everything scrupulously clean. There were some engravings in frames against the wall. Not one of them was an eighth of an inch on one side. There were knitted wool mats on the table; each was exactly at the same distance from the circumference.

When Queenie arrived, she found Grice at the table

with a book open before him. On one side sat Beulah with her hands folded; on the other, Andrew in his glossy black suit, the stiffness and newness of which seemed to have entered into his soul, and glossed and stiffened that. A chair was placed over against Jabez.

"We will seek to improve the occasion," said he. "Will you take that chair?"

Chilled to the heart, with a sense as though an iron hoop were put round her temples and was being tightened, Queenie obeyed, and looked with piteous eyes at the great, solid face opposite.

"Before we begin," said Jabez, "let me call you, Andrew, and you, Beulah, to witness that, on the steps of the New Hall, I shook my umbrella against the Old Field and its skipping-ropes, and butterflies, and pomps."

"Indeed you did, brother. You always testify!" said Beulah with a sigh, opening her hands and then closing them again.

"And I lifted up my voice and prophesied," continued Grice. "I said—Let the earth open her mouth and swallow them up, they and their wives and their children—"

"And Tweedledee," said Andrew. "Indeed, father, it was only Tweedledee that went down."

"I have heard enough of Tweedledee," said Jabez Grice, sternly.

"Oh, brother! what a mercy it was no one but the dog went into the hole!"

"And that's not certain; some think he has been stolen and will turn up after all," added Andrew.

"I said, enough about Tweedledee," said Grice in a loud, commanding tone, and he looked with a dark face at his sister and son. "We will proceed to improve the occasion."

Grice had conceived that there was something more than coincidence in his denunciation of the circus and its immediate collapse. But the response from Andrew and Beulah did not encourage the view, and he said no more thereon.

The chair on which the child was seated was of hard wood—a kitchen chair, with a straight back. At the Rainbow cottage she had been accorded the arm-chair. She was weary, she had hardly closed her eyes the previous night. Her mind had been racked with painful thoughts, her heart full of despair, and now she could not collect her ideas to listen to what was being read or spoken. She strove to keep her dark eyes open and fixed on the massive face of Grice; when so doing she could see and observe nothing save the motion of the black ring of hair about his polished chin.

Then her mind rambled to Heathendom, and she slightly flushed as she recollected that she had left without saying good-bye to, without leaving a message for, Rab Rainbow.

Above the mantleshelf was a picture of Cain killing Abel—a chromo-lithograph glazed. Queenie lifted her eyes to that, but the lids were heavy. She could not long maintain them elevated. Her chair had one leg a little shorter than the others, or else the floor was not quite level. Every now and then involuntarily, with a slight movement of the hard chair, in which she could not rest easily, the leg went down and made a slight noise on the oilcloth that covered the boards. Then she heard Grice's voice pause, and she dared not raise her eyes lest they should encounter his fixed on her in reproof.

Where was Rab? How was it that she had not been able to say a farewell to him?

Then she remembered that the carriage had returned to Saltwich at a very different pace from that at which it had gone to Scatterley. If Rab was walking he had been left some way behind, and he could not arrive at home till after she had left.

Would he be so very cross at her having gone away? She could not have endured to remain longer in that house. Rab was a warm-hearted fellow, but he was no companion for her. He was rough, violent, wild. His mother spoke ill of him, and who would be more inclined to condone a lad's faults than his mother?

This house into which she had been brought—would that be more tolerable than the Rainbows' cottage? Queenie loved tidiness and cleanliness—she was accustomed to both. Her father's house on wheels had been the perfection of neatness. But how different it had been from this house in Alma Terrace. The little compartments of the van had been cosy. By no mental effort could she conceive of cosiness in the room where she now was. This improving discourse surely would not go on interminably! It might last for half an hour. Her head was spinning—possibly it might last an hour. Then she would be suffered to go to bed. She was sleepy, worn out. What sort of room were they going to give her? What sort of bed? Would Mr Grice come up with his great book and read her to sleep?

Her thoughts were becoming confused. She looked again at the picture of the first fratricide, and in her bewildered brain thought that the parts had become reversed, and that Abel was slaughtering Cain, and was knocking him about the head with a great volume. First he knocked his head to one side, then to the other, then he knocked it up with a blow under the chin, then he knocked it down with a blow on the crown.

Queenie's eyes sank to the floor, became dazed, and still saw Abel pounding at Cain with the big book.

She was losing consciousness. To recover herself

she leaned forward, and in so doing altered the centre of gravity of the chair. As the short leg came down, there went a shock through her, and for a moment she was roused. Before her on the table was a wool mat, raised in little flounces of alternate violet and green and red, and at the tip of each little flounce was one steel bead. She timidly put forth a hand to this mat, and took one of the beads between her fingers. She felt its angles, she tried to count them, but could never tell at which she had begun. She was hanging on to consciousness by this one steel bead.

Meanwhile Andrew was watching the poor little girl, white, frail, battling with herself; now with her great eyes wide open, then with them closed, the long, dark lashes sweeping the cheek.

What a little nose she had! Just a bit turned up, just as though it were drawing itself away to allow the lips to be kissed. Andrew blushed as this thought entered his mind.

The golden head had sunk. The chin was buried in the black folds over her bosom. He saw the reflection of the lamp that had been kindled play in waves of fire over the bowed head. The hand had ceased to turn the steel bead. Then the arm fell, and the slender figure of the girl sank together in the chair.

"Andrew!" said his father peremptorily, "where are your eyes?"

The young man recovered himself, and looked at the table.

"Andrew, you'll get no improvement looking at a girl, instead of listening to me. A backslider, a backslider you will be. Never was there an occasion such as this! What have I been speaking about?"

Andrew looked at the sleeping girl, then at his aunt, helplessly.

"I'm sure, father, I don't know."

"You don't know! On such an awful occasion as this! And you cracked nuts when the most famous orator from beyond the Atlantic was haranguing on the undenominational boards."

Then ensued a violent blow at the front door. It was opened from without, and a voice was heard.

"Where is Grice? Where is 'Hammer'? I demand my rights. He has taken her away. She is mine. I will have my rights."

Rab, flushed, partly with anger, partly with drink, stood before them.

"I have come to claim her. She is not yours; she is mine. Give me my rights."

CHAPTER XIII.

NO! NO! NO!

JABEZ GRICE rose slowly from his chair and walked with decided step towards the excited and angry youth.

"You go outside at once!" said he.

Rab looked round the room uncertainly, and encountered the dreamy eyes of Queenie, who had been awakened from her sleep, but had not collected her faculties, and did not understand what was taking place.

"Go out quietly," said Jabez; "do not force me to throw you out."

"Throw me out!" repeated Rab, and looked at the massive man before him.

It was by no means certain that, in a trial of strength, the young man would come best off. He had youth and agility on his side, the other weight and coolness.

Rab said sullenly,—

"I will leave the house if you will come into the garden. I do not wish to frighten *her*."

He pointed with his elbow towards the girl.

"Very well," said Jabez, and strode forward, the young man backing before him, till he was through the door, and in the little garden in front of the house. "Now I am at your service," said "Hammer."

"You know who I am?" asked Rab.

"I have seen you before, Rainbow. What do you want with me?"

"Only a word, 'Hammer.' Stand where the light from the window falls on you, that I may see your face. That will do."

He put out his hand and moved Grice into a position where shone a streak of lamplight.

"You must give her up."

"Give whom up?"

"Oh yes! do not pretend not to understand me. You know whom I mean—the Queen of Love."

"I know no Queen of Love. If you mean Miss Sant, I will trouble you to speak of her in proper terms."

"As if I did not know her before you did! Did she ever give you a yaller rose? Have you ever carried her in your arms? Did you ever save her from death?"

"She is under my protection, and I will protect her from drunken and profligate ruffians."

"And who will protect her from you?" asked Rab. "I do not trust you."

"Not trust me?"

Jabez rose an inch and expanded two. That disreputable fellow did not trust him—him whom all Saltwich trusted, him whom it delighted to elect to committees, whom it made treasurer to clubs, secretary to societies, whom the member trusted at an election, whom the shareholders trusted to let the pews in the chapel, whom Brundrith trusted in the conduct of the Salt Works! It concerned Jabez little that this lout should not share the general confidence. What was the opinion of one man, and he a ne'er-do-weel, against the current of estimation in which he stood?

"Do you know what I did?" asked Rab. "I saved little Queenie's life. She got her life fust from her parents. She got her life agin from me. Therefore I have now the right over her that once had father and mother. But for me she would ha' been trampled under foot, crushed by the tent pole, would ha' been burnt by the oil, smothered in the canvas, perhaps swallered up in the ground. I saved her. I saw her fall from the horses. When everyone else was flyin'—all thinkin' of themselves, how to escape the staggerin' tent and the gapin' earth, then I sprang to where Queenie lay. I took her up. I carried her away." He pulled out his clasp knife and opened it. "Look at this — with this I cut a way out in the great smash up. I carried her through and over it all, and never let go till I had brought her to my home. So she is mine!"

The fellow, in his excitement, gesticulated with the knife.

"Shut that and put it away!" said Jabez. "A tongue suffices wherewith to talk."

"I did all that," said the young man, obeying the command. "And so I say that she belongs to me who gave to her her sweet life. But for me she'd have been buried to-day alongside of her father. If she has eyes wherewith to see—she owes 'em to me. If she can still speak and hear—it is because of me. I gave her speech and hearin', after they had gone from her."

"You behaved, no doubt, in a courageous and unselfish manner," said Grice. "But, after all, you did only what was your duty, what any other man, worth the name of a man, would have done."

"Who did it but I? Every one else was thinkin' how to get out. No one had a care for the poor little Queen of Love, that lay as one dead on the sawdust. No one else jumped the barrier. The clown was concerned only for his dog. The Queen is mine, and I will have her back."

"This is absurd. The girl remains with me. I am her guardian."

'Who made you that?"

"Her father—my brother."

Rab was silent, for a moment perplexed.

"You gave her to me," he said after a while.

"I—I gave her to you?"

"Yes—when her father was dying you said, 'Take her away!'"

Grice laughed.

"You have been drinking, or you would not talk such nonsense. If you have any charge to make for what you have done, put it down on paper and bring me your account. If the bill be reasonable I will settle it, and so have done with you.

Rab did not hear or pay attention to these words. He proceeded:—

"She threw her arms round me when her father was dead. She knew she had no one else to go to—none who would so care for her and protect her so jealously as I—and she threw herself then round my heart, and none can tear her away from that hold."

"I am ready to praise and reward you for what you have done."

"I don't want your reward and I despise your praise," retorted Rab. "Give me up my Queenie—I must take her back."

"I do not acknowledge any right in you over her."

"You think I am a good-for-nothing chap. Well, I won't say but I have been a bit wild. I'm not to be trusted with the little Queenie—there, you don't know me. I'd never hurt a hair of her head, never look at her but as to my Queen; I'd watch about her that no harm should come to her. I'd think how I might make her happy. I'd work to find her all she wanted. She'd be safe enough with me. I'm not so sartain she'll be cared for and considered the same way by you. Yes, I've not been good for much, and mother always says I'm a trial to her. She's gone the wrong way to work to mend me. But Queenie can do with me what she wills. There is my sister married respectably to one o' the head-rangers in Delamere, and my brother-in-law—it's a lot of trouble and vexation I've given him, sure enough—he always says he'll get me an under-keeper's place if I like to take it. I've loved my freedom too much to accept that. But now, give me back little Queen of Love and I'll take the place he offers, and I'll live as decent as a chap can. I won't drink, I won't swear."

"It is of no use your talking, Rainbow. Promises are the most untrustworthy of coin. Performance is the sterling metal."

"Then try me?"

"I have nothing to do with you. The child is my

ward and I shall act as her guardian. Neither you nor any one else shall take her away."

"Let me see her," said Rab.

"Here am I," said Queenie, standing in the doorway with her lame foot resting against the other, and her hand to one of the jambs for her support. "What do you want with me, Rab?"

"Come here! Come to me, little one!" said the young fellow passionately, extending both his arms.

"I cannot, Rab, I am lame."

"Lean on me. I cannot speak before 'Hammer.' Let me take you ten steps—one to me, eight up and down, and one back—if go from me you must. Lean your hand on my shoulder. I will hold you up, and we will have it out, with no 'Hammer' Grice standing by."

She let go the door-post and stepped to him at once.

"You see!" shouted Rab, "Queenie ain't afraid of me. Queenie can trust me—the good-for-naught."

He put his arm round her waist and the girl rested her hand on his shoulder.

"Go in," said he to Jabez Grice. "We two don't want none to hearken—what is between her and me is for us alone, and we want none to look on."

He waited till Grice had retired into the house, but Jabez would not shut the door.

"Now throw your weight upon me, Queen of Love,"

said the young poacher. "Those people in there will make you serious; they'll take the laugh from your lips, and wipe the light out o' your eyes. They won't make you happy. Do not go back to them. One. When you've done the eight little trips, let me take you up in my arms and carry you away."

Pausing on one foot, leaning on his shoulder, the girl turned her head and answered,—

"Indeed, Rab, that cannot be. My father gave me to them. It was his wish—I must obey him."

"Two!" said the young man. "It must out. Thunder and blazes! I can't be silent. I love you, Queenie, I cannot bear to hold it in no longer. I love you!"

"You have been good to me," replied the girl, slightly loosening her hold of his shoulder. "I must always thank you for what you have done for me."

"Thanks! I want no thanks! 'Hammer' says I did what any other man would do. 'Hammer' offered me money, gave me praise. I threw them away. I want love! Three."

"Oh! Rab, don't tease me. I am only a little girl. I give you my gratitude."

"I am not content with that. Four! See! I mean all fair and right. Lord! If anyone had said last week that Rab Rainbow would lose his wits because of a girl, I'd not have believed him. I would have said, 'Let the hares first run after the sportsman, and the sun rise in the west.' I can't help it, it is so!"

"Do not tease me, Rab dear; let me alone. You are asking what I cannot give. I am a child. Then think, Rab, you have no honest profession. You do nothing to earn a livelihood. You idle about, you drink, you swear, and poach!"

"Five. Do not let go your hold of me. I have a will. I will mend my idle, my evil ways. I will get work, honest work; I will work hard. I will never enter a public-house again."

"I would do much for you, Rab."

"Then be mine. Six. I will go to the parson to-morrow and put in the banns, then you needn't stay in this house."

"No, Rab, no! Don't tease me. I can't help it; I must say it—No!"

"Seven. You cast me from you?"

"I do not that. I shall ever regard you as a dear friend, ever respect you, if with a good will you mend your ways. Will not that suffice? Do not tease me. I am a child. I cannot hold to you closer than I do now."

"Then let us go through the world as we are."

She loosed her hold altogether and stumbled to the rails of the little garden and hung to them.

"Let me alone, Rab; you are too good to torment me. I give you what I can—my friendship."

He stood in front of her, and folded his arms and looked hard at her.

"There will mischief come of this. I cannot help it. I am a fellow who must have his way. There will come mischief of this somehow. How, I know not, but I feel it, like a thunderstorm comin' on. Oh, Queenie! do you put me from you? That will be bad for some—bad—worst of all, for me!"

CHAPTER XIV

BEGGAR-MY-NEIGHBOUR

QUEENIE was not uncomfortable in No. 4 Alma Terrace. On the contrary, she was well lodged, well clothed, and well fed; and were human happiness assured by these three points of satisfaction, she would have been content. She had no longer to endure the irritation of the fussy interference of Mrs Rainbow, was no longer maddened by her incessant chatter; thus her overstrung nerves were given the repose they needed. And precisely so long as that was necessary was No. 4 Alma Terrace a place suitable for her. But no sooner had she recovered from her depression, than she found No. 4 Alma Terrace to be a place too strait for her, and its atmosphere not at all congenial.

As George Herbert well said, everlasting droppings young hearts can leastwise bear, and Queenie's mind was not one of the harebell order, but rather of that of the daisy, that holds up its face and drinks in the sun.

The twinkle came back into her eye, her droll little mouth began to curl on one side, all the flash and ripple returned to her glowing hair, and a tinge of colour painted her cheek. As there is spirit in wine, so was there fire in her blood; and in No. 4 Alma Terrace not only was alcohol forbidden in all drinks, but the life-blood was supposed to flow without passion, to produce no intoxicating effect when it rushed to heart or brain. Queenie had nearly the entire day to herself, for Jabez Grice and his son went to their work early, usually before six, and returned after four in the afternoon, when the pans had been cleared of their salt, or, if the boiling continued night and day, they returned when the day gang left and the night gang came on.

Only Beulah was in the house with Queenie for ten hours, and Beulah, though a good woman, was not an interesting one. She sighed over her work, not because she had a grief at heart, not because the work was too much for her, but because to sigh became her profession as an eminently-serious woman. She was a machine, performing her household duties regularly and well; she had but one absorbing idea, which was that her brother was the best and greatest of men. Queenie, unable to endure solitude, accompanied Beulah about the house, assisted her in her work, tried to make the good woman laugh, attempted a romp, and failed in all her attempts. Of entertainment to be got out of Beulah, there was none.

When Andrew and his father returned to the house, the girl tried her powers on the elder man. She drew a stool to his feet, and sat there whilst he read and smoked, pleaded for a whiff of his pipe, a peep at the pictures in his magazine. A little adroit flattery, a little coquettishness got him to unbend for a while, and make some clumsy attempts at humour, but he always became doubly grave and absorbed in his reading after such relaxation. Jabez was, however, not much at home. He returned from the Salt Works to "fettle" a bit, put on his better suit, and then went forth to a committee meeting, or a political debating society, or else occupied himself with accounts at home, when no noise, no talking, hardly a whisper was tolerated in the room.

Andrew formed a more congenial companion for the girl. He was at home when his father was out, and then she had the field to herself. She liked Andrew; not only was he a very good-looking fellow, but his simplicity, his shyness, his ignorance of all the brighter side of life, amused and stimulated the little creature. She delighted in saying startling things, expressing novel opinions, telling droll anecdotes that made Andrew's eyes open and his mouth drop. She was to him a daily astonishment. She bewildered whilst fascinating him. He was in a flutter of doubt whether he was not wrong in liking her, wrong in listening to her, wrong in allowing her to lead him on to trifle and play and waste time, which is too precious to be spent otherwise than in getting up missionary statistics, or assimilating food for serious meditation.

She had extracted from him the story of the nuts at the undenominational meeting, and was incessantly poking fun at him thereupon, sometimes before his father, usually when they were alone together.

She had not been a fortnight in the house before she had upset the salt—put the fat in the fire. The occasion was this:—

"Where are you off to, Andrew?" she asked, one evening, when the youth came down, dressed to go out.

"There's a lecture on Behemoth, at the Young Men's Serious Association."

"Behemoth—who is he?"

"It is an animal."

"I never saw it in any menagerie."

"No; I don't think it has ever been caught. I question if it has ever been seen."

"Never mind about Behemoth. If there were one alive, and the lecturer would show him in a bath, like a talking seal, and if it would say papa and mamma, I'd go. But only to hear a lecture—bah!"

"I think my father would wish me to attend."

"He has not ordered you to go and hear about Behemoth?"

"No; not exactly. He takes it for granted that I will go."

"Don't."

"I may never have another opportunity of hearing and learning about Behemoth."

"What does that matter? If he has never been caught, never seen nor heard nor smelt, I don't suppose the lecturer knows much that is reliable about the animal. You stay with me. Aunt Beulah will go to Behemoth, and we will have rare larks together I'll teach you something better than about Behemoth.'

"What's that?"

"You won't tell?"

"Honour bright."

Queenie crept to his side and whispered,—

"Beggar-my-neighbour."

"Beggar-my-neighbour! I never heard of it."

"Now, Andrew, choose—Behemoth or beggar-my-neighbour."

She put herself in a coaxing attitude, with her head on one side, her eyes half closed, full of malice, and the dimples deepening every moment in her delicate, rosy cheeks.

Andrew threw his cap into the corner of the room.

"Beulah is gone already," said he.

"So much the better; we'll make a night of it."

After a little consideration—"Andrew, have you any money?"

"Yes; a few coppers."

"So have I. I have that very shilling you gave me for the ticket you never used. Go out and buy some chestnuts, toffee and ginger-pop. We'll toast the chestnuts, suck the toffee and be jolly. Blow Behemoth!"

"Queenie! for shame! Don't say such awful words."

"It's not swearing," protested the girl. "Now run and get the chestnuts, toffee and pop. I'll get the other things ready."

"What things?"

"Cards, Andrew—cards."

The young fellow was aghast.

"Cards are sinful," he said, when he recovered from his dismay. "I can't stand this; I'll go to Behemoth."

"You shall not go, Andrew. Behemoth has already been trotted out. It would be bad manners and bad example to go late."

Then she used all her witchery to appease his alarm, to satisfy his conscience, and to excite his curiosity.

The lamp was lighted, the fire was burning, and on the hob the chestnuts were toasting. Now and then one popped and shot across the room. Then there ensued a scramble for it, and they knocked heads together under the table; or, as it burnt the hands of Queenie when she pounced on it, she tossed it to Andrew, who also let it go.

"We'll have a feast after the first round," said the girl, and she rapidly dealt out the cards.

"Mind, four for an ace."

"What's an ace?"

"A one, softie! Three for a king, two for a queen, one for a jack."

"A jack?"

"Yes, that little fellow with legs. The king has none and has a golden crown. Look—the queen has got a yellow rose, and I gave one"—she checked herself and coloured.

"To whom? Not to me."

"No—not to you—I'll give you one when I get it, but I have no rose-garden. Now begin."

For the first time in his life Andrew played a game of chance. Beggar-my-neighbour is not an engrossing game to experienced card-players, but to children, to a youth who had never touched cardboard before, it is what a bull-fight is to a Spaniard, a gladiatorial show to a Roman, what roast pig was to the first Chinaman who tasted it. Andrew's cheeks flamed, he shouted, he grabbed at the cards when he made a set, he trembled when his pictures were swept away. He stood up in his excitement, watching Queenie's cards; he sat down with a bounce. He held his breath whilst Queenie counted out, "one—two—three, jack" to his ace. He groaned and flung himself back in his chair, when against her knave he was able to produce only a three.

Then there came a run of luck against him, and he was reduced to one picture card. But that one retrieved his fortunes. He cleared Queenie's hand out, and had started up with a cry of "Beggared!" when the door opened and in the doorway stood "Hammer" Grice.

Mr Grice had been at the lecture, and was appointed to speak a few words after it. But he found that he had left a little book behind him in which he kept notes, and there were some notes in it relative to Leviathan, who was held to be first cousin to Behemoth, and he returned hastily to No. 4 Alma Terrace for his little book. He stood looking at the card-players with astounded gaze. That this should take place in his house! That his son should be found with cards in his hands! But time was precious!

"Humph!" said "Hammer," and without another word he seized the pack from the unresisting hand of his son, and put it in his pocket. Then he went upstairs, found and pocketed his book of notes. Having done this he left the house.

"Now for the chestnuts and pop," said Queenie.

Andrew was too full of dismay to be able to speak.

He dreaded the consequences too greatly to enjoy the toffee.

Had the matter ended there, it would have been bad enough, but there was a sequel that aggravated it.

Having returned to the meeting and heard the last words of the lecturer relative to Behemoth, Jabez Grice rose to thank the lecturer; and in the course of what he had to say, observed that there were a few facts relative to Leviathan which he had culled in his reading, facts which threw a flood of light upon the manners and habits of Behemoth.

Thereupon he put his hand into his pocket, and drew forth, before a hall full of attentive listeners and eager observers—a pack of cards. Still talking, and not noticing what he had done, Jabez proceeded to say that he would open his notes and read.

Then all at once he saw, staring him in the face, a knave of spades.

The shock was too great for even his iron nerves; his hand trembled, his fingers involuntarily relaxed, and away shot the cards, flying over the platform and snowing upon the audience in the front rows.

But Jabez Grice was not the man to be thrown off his balance for more than a moment by an accident so untoward.

Rapidly recovering his equanimity, in spite of the titters and commotion produced by the showered pack, he said solemnly,—

"The seed of Behemoth. Out of such as this proceeds that monster, *Play*, which consumes our people from the highest to the lowest."

When he came home, it was with his great mouth set hard, and his brows lowering.

Queenie saw that a storm was going to break.

"Oh, uncle," said she, "we have kept some roast chestnuts for you—and—and, as to the cards, we were only *playing* at beggar-my-neighbour."

CHAPTER XV

AGAIN : BEGGAR-MY-NEIGHBOUR

"AUNTIE ! there's a nice little carriage at the door."

Beulah went slowly to the window.

"It is Ada Button ; she who whipped your father's coffin."

There was no necessity for this reference to the past. Queenie would not have recognised either the girl who was driving, or the cob she drove.

There is more mischief done in the world by stupidity than by malice. Beulah was wholly devoid of gall, but she was stupid to her finger-tips, and, because stupid, she said words that never ought to have been spoken, stirred a painful topic that should not have been retouched.

Had little Queenie been resentful and morose—one to harbour wrongs and to seek revenge—this revival of an ugly and distressing incident would have roused her passions. But the little horsemanship girl was of a gentle, forgiving nature, and already, on her way home from the funeral, had reproached herself for having resented an act which her sound sense told her must have been accidental.

Instead of flying into a fit of anger or turning sullen, Queenie said calmly,—

"That is she—is it? I am glad she is come. She has got no whip, only a stick—who is the saddler here in Saltwich?"

"She wants to come in," said Beulah. "There is no one to hold the horse."

"I will do that," said the girl. "I have not patted a horse, I have not spoken to one, since I came here, and I love horses."

Without another word Queenie hopped out at the door and went to the carriage.

"Shall I hold the cob, miss?" she asked.

"Thank you—for a minute."

Miss Button looked hard at the girl, and Queenie stared at her.

Ada Button was tall, with very dark hair and eyes, the latter hard as polished stone and as cold. She had a white face, regular, with thin lips. Altogether she would have been handsome, had not the lower portion of her face been too sharp and the mouth too large for beauty. The face was as stony as the eyes. She had no colour in her cheeks, her lips were too narrow to show strips of rose, and the only tinge of pink discernible in her face was about the nostrils. She had long, narrow hands, and Queenie saw that she had also singularly straight, narrow feet. She observed this as Ada stepped out of the carriage.

"You want to see Aunt Beulah?" she asked.

"Yes; I want to see Miss Grice. Will you drive the cob up and down? He is warm, and the wind is cold. You, I suppose, are the—the—I don't know the name—but you were—"

"The merry little wandering Queen of Love—now I am the moping, sitting-at-home Miss Muffet."

"I suppose you find a change. Dull, perhaps?"

"Awful!" Then thinking she had said an ungracious thing, she added, "They are very kind, but No. 4 Alma Terrace is not a circus. It is not even a menagerie, for they are all of one kind here, and no monkeys, no parrots, only solemn owls. They have been very good to me; it's no fault of theirs that they are not comic. It's their misfortune."

Ada Button put the reins into Queenie's hands, and entered the house. The circus girl went to the horse's head and talked to him, coaxed him, and whispered secrets into his ear. The horse flicked his ears, turned his head and rubbed his nose against her cheek.

"I knew we should be friends," said the girl; "all horses like me. And I'll speak a word for you to your mistress when she comes out, if she gives me the opportunity."

Then she hopped into the carriage.

A quarter of an hour later, when Ada Button issued from the house, she looked up and down the terrace, but could not see the carriage.

"Come inside again," said Beulah; "she's driving about to prevent the horse catching cold."

"She is doing more than drive about," said Ada in a hard tone.

At that moment Queenie was visible flourishing a whip; when she saw that the mistress of the little trap was waiting, she cracked the lash without touching the horse, and came on at a trot. When she drew up, it was with a smiling face and merry eyes.

"There!" said she, "I did wrong the other day. I have bought you a new whip. It cost three-and-six. Take it. I broke the other. But the cob does not want one, he goes very well with a word."

Ada Button drew back.

"You never intended it," said Queenie. "It was quite accidental that you struck father's coffin with your lash."

"Of course, I knew nothing about him, nothing about you. I did not know there was a funeral when I came round the corner. I did not hear the bell. My cob dashed up, and shied."

"There is your whip."

Looking into Ada Button's cold, inflexible face, Queenie noticed a dark mark on the cheek bone

"I hope I did not hurt you when I threw the bits of stick in your face."

"You struck and bruised me."

"I am very sorry; I am, indeed. If you will let me, I will kiss your cheek where I bruised it."

Ada shrank away. She answered coldly,—

"You are good—the injury is nothing. I will not trouble you."

Miss Button entered the carriage and drove away.

Queenie looked after her, shook her head and said,—

"There's not much fun in her, poor thing. But she can't help it. Aunt Beulah, now I'm beggared. I haven't any money left. The saddler wanted four shillings, but I had only three-and-six; as it was ready money, he took it. I must ask uncle for more."

"Ask for more! What can you require money for?"

"You see—I bought a whip."

When, somewhat later, Jabez Grice returned from the Salt Works, and seated himself by the fire, lit his pipe and took his newspaper, Queenie placed herself on a stool near him, and gradually sidled to his knee, laid both her hands on it, and her chin on her hands, and so looked up.

The newspaper was between her and the face of Grice, but Jabez was well aware that the twinkling eyes were fixed on him athwart the sheet—it was as though the fire from them shot through the paper.

For some while he pretended to ignore her, but the consciousness that she was looking and waiting took off his attention from a speech in the House that he was reading. Then, with her forefinger, Queenie began to scratch slightly at his knee, just sufficiently to tickle and tease.

"Well!" said Grice, raising his paper. "What's up?"

"It's all up with my pocket-money, uncle."

"Didn't know you had any."

"Yes, my dear father was so good. He always put up a nest-egg in my pocket. It was never quite empty."

"You want no money."

"Indeed, uncle, I do."

"Yes, indeed, to buy chestnuts and ginger-beer and playing cards. Chestnuts are harmless—ginger-pop is—well it makes for seriousness—but cards are wicked."

"Set the cards against the pop, uncle, and we are squared off."

"You are best without money. Don't bother me."

He lowered the paper.

Queenie was quiet for a few minutes, and then she began to scratch his knee again.

"Come, will you leave my knee-cap alone?"

"Uncle, I spent three-and-six on a whip."

"Where is it? I'll lay it across your shoulders."

"I gave it to Miss Button in place of that I broke."

"It is well; now you cannot get into mischief with money. No more cards."

"No, uncle, but I should like to have a little money. I'm fond of brandy-balls."

"Brandy—what?"

"I do not think there is brandy in them—only peppermint. Some people call them humbugs."

"You are better without them. They will upset you. And besides, I don't choose to have you running about the town into all the shops."

"Oh, uncle, I cannot run; you know I've sprained my ankle."

"Well, hopping about. If you have no money, you will be forced to stay at home; at all events, have no excuse for going out."

"Uncle," said Queenie, and now she laid her cheek on the hands that were crossed on his knee, and her golden hair flowed down over his leg. Her roguish eyes were peering up at him sideways. "Uncle, you have sold the circus horses?"

"Yes"—answered reluctantly.

"Did you sell them well?"

"Middling."

"For how much? They cost father pots of money."

"I really do not carry details in my head."

"And the vans? Our beautiful van with the paintings and the gilded work? Is that sold, too?"

"It is on the way to be sold."

"Will it fetch a tidy price?"

"Middling only."

"And all the properties, have you sold them?"

"Yes, in a lump."

"Did they go off well?"

"Miserably—old rags."

"How much did you get for all together?"

"I really cannot say. The expenses were heavy. I had to pay off all the troupe, and there was the keep of the horses and other beasts till the sale, the advertising, and so on. You do not understand these matters. Take yourself off. Don't peer up at me from under my paper. Don't tickle my knee."

"But I do understand, uncle, and I'm awfully interested in the matter."

"Indeed! Why so?"

"Because it's my money."

"Your money!" Jabez Grice dropped the paper on his knees; in so doing he covered the little head. He noticed this and drew the paper aside. "Your money! Fiddlesticks!"

"I suppose it is mine. Didn't father leave it to me? I'm his child."

Grice was silent. His mouth closed and his brow contracted. Then he said slowly,—

"Understand this, once for all. I am your guardian. Your father put you unreservedly into my hands. Nothing is yours but what I choose to let you have—and mind this, I don't let you have anything which I am quite sure will not be spent profitably and in such a manner as my conscience will allow. I am responsible for your money—I am responsible for you. If you wanted to buy a box of matches wherewith to set fire to your clothes, do you suppose I would let you have it? There is something much more precious than your clothes. I must take care that the money I have in trust—mind me—in trust, is not so spent as to imperil your happiness in this world and the next."

"Five bob, uncle?" coaxingly.

"I do not mind a trifle, but not such a sum as that; and mind—no cards!"

"Pop, uncle, pop!"

Then he gave her a couple of shillings, and resumed his paper.

She turned her head on his knee and looked into the fire. Thus she did not irritate him. She had, moreover, ceased to scratch at his knee.

Presently he said, raising his paper,—

"You are laughing, or crying—which is it? You shake my knee, and that shakes the paper, and I cannot read."

"I am laughing, uncle."

"What at?"

"At you and me."

"Indeed; what is there in me to feed your mirth?"

"Oh, uncle, we are playing at beggar-my-neighbour, you and I—and I am rather afraid I'm going to be cleared out!"

CHAPTER XVI

THE TIGHT-ROPE

THE day was Sunday, the time evening.

Jabez Grice was upstairs washing and burnishing himself for chapel. For this process strong yellow soap and a rough towel were employed. After the process a veritable gloss was over his forehead, cheeks, chin, as though he had been gone over with beeswax and turpentine—even his nose shone. Beulah was arranging herself in her best gown and bonnet, both sober in colour, and getting her hands with difficulty into gloves.

Andrew was ready first. He came down into the sitting-room, in the grate of which no fire burned on the Sunday, to economise labour. Queenie was there standing on one toe.

"Andrew," said the girl, "put down your ear. I want to whisper something—a secret. You won't tell?"

"No; I can keep a secret."

"Put your ear lower. My ankle is better—is all right."

"I am very glad to hear it. Next Sunday you can accompany us to Little Bethel."

Again Queenie put up her mouth.

"Bend your ear again, Andrew. You don't know all."

"What more?"

"I am shamming."

"Oh! Queenie, what for?"

"I don't want to go to chapel."

Andrew pulled himself upright, and drew from her. He was shocked. She knew that what she had said would shock him. That was precisely why she said it.

Presently, down came Mr and Miss Grice in full plumage, with hymn books in their hands.

"You will find improving literature in that cabinet," said Jabez to his niece. "There are some volumes of sermons, a book on prophecy, and—some missionary reports. Occupy yourself seriously and profitably until we return. It is most unfortunate that your ankle is so bad."

Queenie looked out of the corner of her eyes at Andrew, and a dimple formed in her cheek. He became uneasy and shuffled with his feet.

"Now and then, Queenie," said Beulah, "look at

the kitchen fire; see that it is all right, and that there is enough water with the potatoes that are boiling."

"She can take her books with her, and read in the kitchen," said Grice. "Mind, child, no wasting of time. Use the hours in which you might have been with us in something that will do you good."

Then the three left. As Jabez departed, he turned the key in the front door, and then carried it off in his pocket.

"I declare, he has locked me in! That is mean!" said the girl. "I don't care. I can get out by the back yard if I choose, or through the parlour window. And I will!"

As soon as she thought Grice was well on his way to Bethel she threw up the sash and jumped out into the garden in front. The height was but three feet. Then she went forward and sat on the dwarf wall supporting the railings that enclosed the garden, and watched the good people of Alma Terrace go by with their hymn books in hand. After a while the flow of the seriously-disposed ceased. Alma Terrace settled into silence as of death. There was hardly an inmate of the row left behind. Then up came the lamplighter. A gas lamp was in the road immediately in front of No. 4, and the lighter halted at it and turned the tap.

He observed the girl and nodded, paused and said,— "Well, little miss, left alone?"

"Yes—but it's my own doing."

"Waiting for somebody?" asked the lamplighter in a sly tone, winking with an eye and with his lighter at once.

"I don't want somebody. I want everybody," answered she. "It's deadly dull here."

"I suppose it is."

"Awful!"

"Well, I'm sorry I can't stay to keep company with you."

"You're very kind. I'm Queen in name, but a queen without power. Do you know what I would do if I were a real queen?"

"Raise me to share your throne?"

"Not quite that, lamplighter. I'd turn this terrace into a grand parade, like that at Scarborough. And I'd have smart ladies and gentlemen to march up and down; and a shooting-gallery, and a photograph booth, and donkeys to ride, and goat carriages, and soldiers, and everything that is beautiful. Would it not be sweet?"

"That would not suit the Alma Terrace people; they would go off in a swarm and take you with them. Now, good-bye. We'll have another talk together next time I come round. I've got twenty-six more lamps to light before half-past seven."

No. 8 Alma Terrace was the most aristocratic in the whole row—it maintained a whole servant. In the other houses charwomen appeared occasionally to help in the washing, or at a spring cleaning, but No. 8 rejoiced, and puffed itself up with pride, at being in a position to maintain a salaried domestic. This domestic, Mary Jane, had, so she informed her mistress, received a letter to say that her grandmother was dying, and she had asked leave to go that evening and receive the last blessing of the expiring and venerable dame.

After the departure of the lamplighter, the milkboy from Button's came that way in very dapper get-up, with a check waistcoat and a spotted tie, and put his fingers into his mouth and whistled outside No. 8. Thereupon Mary Jane sallied forth in all the gay colours she could muster, and went off accompanied by the milkboy, no doubt to see her dying grandmother.

Now Alma Terrace was completely lifeless, and Queenie was tired of sitting on the dwarf wall and peering between the rails, so she scrambled through the window again into the parlour.

How could she amuse herself? She had the house —she had the whole of Alma Terrace—she had all Jewry to herself.

She put chairs round the table, and proceeded to jump over them, and continued doing this till out of breath. Then she threw herself down in her uncle's chair and panted,—

"What am I to do?"

Should she pull out the serious books, make a circus of them on the table, catch black beetles in the kitchen, and make them run in the improvised circus? No, black beetles smell—are disgusting creatures. If she could be sure of crickets, she would do it. But crickets are not common, nor are they easily captured.

She jumped out of the chair, weary of inaction, ascended the stairs, went into Aunt Beulah's room, dressed herself up in the garments Miss Grice had just taken off, and began to pirouette, curtsey, dance, and make grimaces before the looking-glass. It was infinitely comical in Aunt Beulah's cap, in her stiff gown, and with a certain affectation of the old woman's manner, to go through this outrageous pantomime.

Queenie tired of this amusement. There was no one present to see how droll she was, and it palled on her. She resumed her own gown, went to her box and pulled out her spangled dress—that in which she had last ridden; that in which she had been rescued by Rab.

Then a wave of desolation swept over her heart, and the tears came into her eyes. Oh! the merry days of the circus! Oh! the genial, good-hearted company that had composed the troupe. That funny, tiresome clown, and the routine of locking him up in the monkey cage. The severe and censorious Mrs Nelson—severe and censorious only to her husband, gushing with tenderness to her. And Seth—that vulgar, good, stupid lad. And her father, so cheerful, so fond of her, so exact in all his dealings, so beloved by all who came in contact with him.

Tears fell among the spangles.

Then Queenie jumped up.

"I must not be out of heart," she said. "If I'm not jolly now when they're all out of the house, when can I be jolly? But Andrew is not a bad fellow; one can get fun out of him."

She seated herself on her bed and considered, with her finger to her cheek. How was she to kill time till the return of the Grices?

Queenie thrust both her hands into her hair and held her head as though afraid it were going to roll away from her, so full was it of lively, quicksilver thoughts; and that poor little body, in its black gown, must remain imprisoned in No. 4 Alma Terrace.

What nonsense it was of Uncle Grice to lock the door! Did he think that it would not be possible for her to get out through the window? Or did he lock it so as to prevent anyone coming in? Who but Rab was to come? She would hardly have let him in by the door, and she most assuredly would not admit him by the window.

"I do wonder," said Queenie, "when I am a little more grown up and am wiser, whether I shall be able to earn my own livelihood, and so not have to stay always in deadly dull Alma Terrace? I could go jumping about on the flat saddles upon horses in a circus. There's no great art in that. I wonder whether I could dance on a tight-rope? That would be an accomplishment."

It occurred to her that there was a very stout cord in an outhouse in the back yard.

There would be no harm in trying if she could steady herself—she had run round on the barrier about the circus often, and had not tumbled. Why would it be more difficult on a rope, and on one stretched in a direct line?

There would be no harm in trying. If she failed, she failed. If she could manage it, then she might practise again till perfect.

But where could the rope be strained?

There was the lamp-post, there were the railings. It could be fastened across the garden, and at no great elevation above the grass, so that she would incur no risk. But how make it firm at the other end? Alma Terrace was deserted, and would be a solitude till the chapels disgorged—and that would not be for an hour.

She descended from her room, went to the outhouse and dragged the rope indoors, into the parlour.

She went to the window, drawing it after her. Yes, the lamp-post would serve famously as a strainer. It was not possible to fasten the other end to the water-pipe that drained the rain from the roof. She could not have passed the cord between it and the brick wall. If there was anything in the room to which she might fasten the rope, then it would pass over the window-sill, and that would be like the bridge of a fiddle—help to hold the cord in position, and precisely at the right height above the soil. The chiffonier would not answer; it occupied the space between the window and the wall.

Of course—the bars of the grate. There was no fire burning! Nothing could serve her purpose better. There were three strong steel bars; she would make a noose and attach the rope to them. They would never give way; then the line would pass under the table and out at the window that was immediately opposite the fireplace, and so in direct course to the lamp-post. She went down on her knees and fastened the cord to the bars of the grate, crawled with it under the table, popped out with the end in her hand over the window-sill, and heard an exclamation of—"Queen of Love!"

"Oh, Rab! This is famous! Oh, I am so glad!"

She dropped her end of rope, and ran through the garden to the young poacher and shook hands with him athwart the railings.

"Queenie! I thought you might be at home, and I have brought you something."

"You good Rab. What is it?"

"Your silver wings! They were bent and bruised. You left them at mother's; I have been trying my hand at them." In a low and doubtful tone—"It was a labour of love, Queenie," then, in his ordinary voice he proceeded,—"I straightened the wires and, with the help of mother's needle and flat-iron, I have got them to look as well as they did when on your back."

"Oh! you dear Rab, you are a beauty!"

"I am neither one nor the other—not to you," said the young man in a tone of dissatisfaction. "I wish I were. But I thought I might give you a pleasure, and it kept my hands out of mischief. So I have put them to rights, and here they are!"

He held out the little wings, and fluttered them in the night air, and in the light from the gas lamp.

"Oh, Rab, you are a good old boy!" She took her wings and capered for joy. "Rab, I want you to help me. I can't do what I wish myself. I am going to try a little tight-rope dancing. I have fastened the cord inside—it is quite firm, a slip-knot to the steel bars of the grate—but I do not think I should be strong enough, alone, to make the other end firm to the lamp-post."

"I will do that for you, as well as I can. Pass me

the poker and I'll use that as a twister. I'll get the cord taut."

"Rab, it wouldn't be proper for me to go on the tight-rope in my mourning black—would it?"

"I suppose not; put on the wings."

"I'll do more. Whilst you are tightening the cord, I'll go up and dress in my spangles and muslin. I have got a balancing-pole out of the back yard—one of the stretchers Aunt Beulah uses for the line on which she hangs the clothes after Monday's washing."

Queenie departed, and was absent for about a quarter of an hour, during which time Rab had done his utmost to strain the rope.

When she returned to the parlour, she was in her muslin, and had adjusted the wings to her back. A lamp burned in the little front sitting-room. The girl had to stoop under the sash to get through the window. Outside, there was a ledge on which she could stand upright.

"Is all ready, Rab?"

"As ready as I can make it."

"Rab, I shall never do it without music."

"I cannot get together a band."

"You can whistle, and hammer on a tea-tray."

"I haven't got a tray."

"You shall have one in a minute."

Queenie dived back into the parlour, and presently reappeared with Aunt Beulah's best japanned tray;

she jumped into the garden, ran across the sod, and passed the tray out to the young man, who at once seated himself on the dwarf wall, and began to pipe between his lips, and strike his knuckles against the metal.

The girl ran back to the window, assumed her balancing-pole and mounted the ledge.

She took one step. Then a second.

The rope bowed under her. She righted herself; took a third, then quickly another, and down she went with the rope upon the sward.

The fall was inconsiderable. She was not in the least hurt.

"Oh, Rab," said she, "something has given way. I have not pulled over the lamp-post? No—nor broken the rails. It must be at the other end."

She went to the window, and, leaning her elbows on the sill, looked in. The rope lay loose on the turf of the garden, slack over the window sill, and limp on the floor of the parlour.

She turned her head over her shoulder, and signed to Rab to come to her.

He opened the garden gate, and joined her at the window, put his hand over his eyes and looked in.

"Rab," said Queenie solemnly, "here's a go!"

"Rather!" responded he, gravely.

"What is to be done?"

"Nothing."

"I shall catch it."

"He will not dare to strike you?"

"Oh no!—not that, but he will look—awful! And he will speak—awful! I should prefer smacks."

What Rab and Queenie saw was this—the strain of the rope, with the additional weight of the girl, had not indeed broken the bars, but had pulled the entire grate out of its place, over the fender, and had precipitated it into the middle of the room, which was strewn with coal; whilst the hearth was cavernous, ruinous. A mass of broken bricks, mortar and soot was heaped on it and scattered over the hearth-rug.

The two young people looked at the wreckage in dismay. What Rab had said was true—nothing whatever could be done by them, nothing could be done till the morrow, and then masons must be called in.

The two were both leaning on the sill, looking into the room—Rab in his rough and untidy fustian, his shabby cap at the back of his head, gaiters on his calves. Queenie was in her fairy costume, the wings fluttering at her back.

Thus they stood dismayed at what had been done, and both dreading the consequences; Rab regretting that he could not relieve his little companion of them, when they were startled by voices in their rear on the pathway before the terrace.

The congregations in the chapels had dissolved, all the serious were on their way home.

Those who came first were arrested—some by the cord stretching from the lamp-post to the rail, others by the astounding picture before them at the parlour window of No. 4!—save the mark, of No. 4!

So astonished were they that they could not speak. More arrived, a little knot was formed and increased.

Then came Jabez—he looked, dashed the garden gate open, strode through to the window, grasped Queenie by the shoulder, and said in quivering tones,—

"What is the meaning of this? Good Heavens! if I had taken a rhinoceros to my bosom it might have proved more inconvenient, it could not have occasioned one-thousandth part of the scandal caused by this dreadful girl!"

END OF VOL. I.

COLSTON AND COMPANY, PRINTERS, EDINBURGH.

A LIST OF NEW BOOKS AND ANNOUNCEMENTS OF METHUEN AND COMPANY PUBLISHERS : LONDON 36 ESSEX STREET W.C.

CONTENTS

	PAGE
FORTHCOMING BOOKS,	2
POETRY,	8
GENERAL LITERATURE,	9
THEOLOGY,	12
LEADERS OF RELIGION,	14
WORKS BY S. BARING GOULD,	14
FICTION,	16
NOVEL SERIES,	19
BOOKS FOR BOYS AND GIRLS,	20
THE PEACOCK LIBRARY,	21
UNIVERSITY EXTENSION SERIES,	22
SOCIAL QUESTIONS OF TO-DAY,	23
COMMERCIAL SERIES,	24

APRIL 1894

April 1894.

Messrs. Methuen's
SPRING ANNOUNCEMENTS

Gale. CRICKET SONGS. By NORMAN GALE. *Crown 8vo. Linen.* 2s. 6d. *net.*
Also a limited edition on hand-made paper. *Demy 8vo.* 10s. 6d. *net.*
Also a small edition on Japanese paper. *Demy 8vo.* 21s. *net.*

Mr. Gale's rural poems have made him widely popular, and this volume of spirited verse will win him a new reputation among the lovers of our national game.

Flinders Petrie. THE HISTORY OF EGYPT, FROM THE EARLIEST TIMES TO THE HYKSOS. By W. M. FLINDERS PETRIE, Professor of Egyptology at University College. *Fully Illustrated. Crown 8vo.* 6s.

This volume is the first of a History of Egypt in six volumes, intended both for students and for general reading and reference, and will present a complete record of what is now known, both of dated monuments and of events, from the prehistoric age down to modern times. For the earlier periods every trace of the various kings will be noticed, and all historical questions will be fully discussed.

The special features will be—

(1) The illustrations, largely photographic, or from *fac-simile* drawings; and, so far as practicable, of new material not yet published. As yet, there is no illustrated history of Egypt;

(2) The references given to the source of each statement and monument, making this a key to the literature of the subject;

(3) The lists of all the known monuments of each king;

(4) The incorporation of current research down to the present time.

The volumes will cover the following periods;—

I. Prehistoric to Hyksos times. By Prof. Flinders Petrie.
II. XVIIIth to XXth Dynasties.   (The Same).
III. XXIst to XXXth Dynasties.   (The Same).
IV. The Ptolemaic Rule.
V. The Roman Rule.
VI. The Muhammedan Rule.   By Stanley Lane Poole.

The volumes will be issued separately. The first will be ready in the autumn, the Muhammedan volume early next year, and others at intervals of half a year.

Ottley. LANCELOT ANDREWES, Bishop of Winchester. A Biography. By R. L. OTTLEY, Principal of Pusey House, Oxford, and Fellow of Magdalen. *With Portrait. Crown 8vo. Buckram.* 5s.

This life of the saintly bishop and theologian, of whom no adequate biography exists, will have much value for English Churchmen. It is issued uniform with Mr. Lock's 'Life of Keble,' and written as it is by so distinguished a scholar as Mr. Ottley, it is as likely to become as popular.

Gladstone. THE SPEECHES AND PUBLIC ADDRESSES OF THE RT. HON. W. E. GLADSTONE, M.P. With Notes. Edited by A. W. HUTTON, M.A. (Librarian of the Gladstone Library), and H. J. COHEN, M.A. With Portraits. *8vo. Vol. IX.* 12s. 6d.

Messrs. METHUEN beg to announce that they are about to issue, in ten volumes 8vo, an authorised collection of Mr. Gladstone's Speeches, the work being undertaken with his sanction and under his superintendence. Notes and Introductions will be added.

In view of the interest in the Home Rule Question, it is proposed to issue Vols. IX. and X., which will include the speeches of the last seven or eight years, immediately, and then to proceed with the earlier volumes. Volume X. is already published.

Robbins. THE EARLY LIFE OF WILLIAM EWART GLADSTONE. By A. F. ROBBINS. *Crown 8vo.* 6s.

A full account of the early part of Mr. Gladstone's extraordinary career, based on much research, and containing a good deal of new matter, especially with regard to his school and college days.

Henley and Whibley. A BOOK OF ENGLISH PROSE. Collected by W. E. HENLEY and CHARLES WHIBLEY. *Crown 8vo.* Also small limited editions on Dutch and Japanese paper. 21s. and 42s. *net.*

A companion book to Mr. Henley's well-known 'Lyra Heroica.' It is believed that no such collection of splendid prose has ever been brought within the compass of one volume. Each piece, whether containing a character-sketch or incident, is complete in itself. The book will be finely printed and bound.

Beeching. BRADFIELD SERMONS. Sermons by H. C. BEECHING, M.A., Rector of Yattendon, Berks. *Crown 8vo.* 2s. 6d.

Six sermons preached before the boys of Bradfield College.

Parkyn. CHARLES DARWIN: a Lecture delivered at Christ's College, Cambridge, by E. A. PARKYN, M.A. *Crown 8vo.* 1s.

A short account of the work and influence of Darwin.

MESSRS. METHUEN'S LIST

Waldstein. JOHN RUSKIN: a Study. By CHARLES WALD-STEIN, M.A., Fellow of King's College, Cambridge. *Post 8vo.* 5s.
Also a small edition on hand-made paper. *Demy 8vo.* 15s.

This is a frank and fair appreciation of Mr. Ruskin's work and influence—literary and social—by an able critic, who has enough admiration to make him sympathetic, and enough discernment to make him impartial.

Sterne. TRISTRAM SHANDY. By LAWRENCE STERNE. With an Introduction by CHARLES WHIBLEY, and a Portrait. 2 *vols. Crown 8vo.* 7s.

Congreve. THE COMEDIES OF WILLIAM CONGREVE. Edited, with an Introduction by G. S. STREET, and a Portrait. *Crown 8vo.* 3s. 6d.

The above important editions of two English classics are finely printed by Messrs. Constable, and handsomely bound. Each is carefully edited with scholarly introductions—biographical and critical. They are issued in two editions—
The ordinary edition on laid paper, bound in buckram, 3s. 6d. a volume.
The library edition (limited in number) on hand-made paper, bound in half parchment, 7s. 6d. a volume, net.

UNIVERSITY EXTENSION SERIES

NEW VOLUMES. Crown 8vo. 2s. 6d.

THE EARTH. An Introduction to Physiography. By EVAN SMALL, M.A.

Methuen's Commercial Series

NEW VOLUMES.

A PRIMER OF BUSINESS. By S. JACKSON, M.A. 1s. 6d.
COMMERCIAL ARITHMETIC. By F. G. TAYLOR, M.A.
THE ECONOMICS OF COMMERCE. By H. de B. GIBBINS, M.A. 1s. 6d.

SOCIAL QUESTIONS OF TO-DAY

NEW VOLUMES. Crown 8vo. 2s. 6d.

WOMEN'S WORK. By LADY DILKE, MISS BULLEY, and MISS ABRAHAM.

TRUSTS, POOLS AND CORNERS. As affecting Commerce and Industry. By J. STEPHEN JEANS, M.R.I., F.S.S.

THE FACTORY SYSTEM. By R. COOKE TAYLOR.

THE STATE AND ITS CHILDREN. By GERTRUDE TUCKWELL.

Classical Translations

NEW VOLUMES.

Crown 8vo. Finely printed and bound in blue buckram.

LUCIAN—Six Dialogues (Nigrinus, Icaro-Menippus, Cock, Ship, Parasite, Law of Falsehood). Translated by S. T. IRWIN, M.A., Assistant Master at Clifton; late Scholar of Lincoln College, Oxford.

SOPHOCLES—Electra and Ajax. Translated by E. D. A. MORSHEAD, M.A., late Scholar of New College, Oxford; Assistant Master at Winchester.

TACITUS—Agricola and Germania. Translated by R. B. TOWNSHEND, late Scholar of Trinity College, Cambridge.

CICERO—Select Orations (Pro Milone, Pro Murena, Philippic II., In Catilinam). Translated by H. E. D. BLAKISTON, M.A., Fellow and Tutor of Trinity College, Oxford.

Fiction

E. F. Benson. THE RUBICON. By E. F. BENSON, Author of 'Dodo.' 2 vols. *Crown 8vo.* 21s.

The announcement of a new novel of society by the author of the brilliantly successful 'Dodo' will excite great interest, and it is believed that 'The Rubicon' will prove to have as much fascination as its predecessor.

Stanley Weyman. UNDER THE RED ROBE. By STANLEY WEYMAN, Author of 'A Gentleman of France,' etc. With 12 Illustrations by R. CATON WOODVILLE. 2 vols. *Crown 8vo.* 21s.

Mr. Weyman's fine historical tales have placed him in the front rank of novelists, and this stirring story of Richelieu and the Huguenots will not lessen his reputation.

Mrs. Oliphant. THE PRODIGALS. By Mrs. OLIPHANT. 2 *vols. Crown 8vo.* 21*s.*

It is hardly necessary to say much about a new story from Mrs. Oliphant's graceful pen. The present one is a charming and pathetic study.

Baring Gould. THE QUEEN OF LOVE. By S. BARING GOULD, Author of 'Mehalah,' 'Cheap Jack Zita,' etc. 3 *vols. Crown 8vo.* 31*s.* 6*d.*

A story of the Cheshire salt region—a new district for the exercise of Mr. Baring Gould's original and powerful gifts.

Gilbert Parker. THE TRANSLATION OF A SAVAGE. By GILBERT PARKER, Author of 'Pierre and His People,' 'Mrs. Falchion,' etc. *Crown 8vo.* 5*s.*

A story with a powerful and pathetic motive by a writer who has rapidly made his way to the front.

Richard Pryce. WINIFRED MOUNT. By RICHARD PRYCE, Author of 'Miss Maxwell's Affections,' 'Time and the Woman,' etc. 2 *vols. Crown 8vo.* 21*s.*

A story of society by Mr. Pryce, whose clever pen has the lightness and ease of Octave Feuillet.

C. Smith. A CUMBERER OF THE GROUND. By CONSTANCE SMITH, Author of 'The Riddle of Lawrence Haviland.' 3 *vols. Crown 8vo.* 31*s.* 6*d.*

Carew. JIM B.: a Story. By F. S. CAREW. *Cr. 8vo.* 2*s.* 6*d.*

S. O'Grady. THE COMING OF CURCULAIN. By STANDISH O'GRADY, Author of 'Finn and His Companions,' 'The Story of Ireland,' etc. *Crown 8vo.* 2*s.* 6*d.*

Curculain is one of the great legendary heroes of the Irish, and the adventures of his early life are told by Mr. O'Grady in his brilliant and fascinating manner.

NEW AND CHEAPER EDITIONS

Marie Corelli. BARABBAS : A DREAM OF THE WORLD'S TRAGEDY. By MARIE CORELLI, Author of 'A Romance of Two Worlds,' 'Vendetta,' etc. *Seventh Edition. Crown 8vo.* 6*s.*

A cheaper edition of a book which aroused in some quarters more violent hostility than any book of recent years. By most secular critics the authoress was accused of bad taste, bad art, and gross blasphemy; but in curious contrast, most of the religious papers acknowledged the reverence of treatment and the dignity of conception which characterised the book. Of this cheaper issue the fourth, fifth, and sixth editions were sold on publication.

MESSRS. METHUEN'S LIST

Baring Gould. CHEAP JACK ZITA. By S. BARING GOULD.
Crown 8vo. 6s.
A cheap edition of a story which has been recognised as Mr. Baring Gould's most original effort since 'Mehalah.'

Fenn. THE STAR GAZERS. By G. MANVILLE FENN.
Crown 8vo. 3s. 6d.
An exciting story with many sensations, and a complex plot.

Esmé Stuart. A WOMAN OF FORTY. By ESMÉ STUART.
Crown 8vo. 3s. 6d.
Pathetic in motive, with an admirably worked out plot, and without overmuch analysis of character, the book has won much praise and many readers.

Educational

Davis. TACITI GERMANIA. Edited with Notes and Introduction. By R. F. DAVIS, M.A., Editor of the 'Agricola.' *Small crown 8vo.*

Stedman. GREEK TESTAMENT SELECTIONS. Edited by A. M. M. STEDMAN, M.A. *Third and Revised Edition. Fcap. 8vo.* 2s. 6d.

Stedman. STEPS TO FRENCH. By A. M. M. STEDMAN, M.A. 18mo.
An attempt to supply a very easy and very short book of French Lessons.

Stedman. A VOCABULARY OF LATIN IDIOMS AND PHRASES. *Fcap. 8vo.*

Malden. ENGLISH RECORDS: A COMPANION TO ENGLISH HISTORY. By H. E. MALDEN, M.A. *Crown 8vo.*

PRIMARY CLASSICS

A series of Classical Readers, Edited for Lower Forms with Introductions, Notes, Maps, and Vocabularies.

Herodotus. THE PERSIAN WARS. Edited by A. G. LIDDELL, M.A., Assistant Master at Nottingham High School. 18mo. 1s. 6d.

Livy. THE KINGS OF ROME. Edited by A. M. M. STEDMAN, M.A. 18mo. *Illustrated.* 1s. 6d.

Caesar. THE HELVETIAN WAR. Edited by A. M. M. STEDMAN, M.A. 18mo. 1s.

New and Recent Books

Poetry

Rudyard Kipling. BARRACK-ROOM BALLADS; And Other Verses. By RUDYARD KIPLING. *Seventh Edition. Crown 8vo.* 6s.

A Special Presentation Edition, bound in white buckram, with extra gilt ornament. 7s. 6d.

'Mr. Kipling's verse is strong, vivid, full of character. . . . Unmistakable genius rings in every line.'—*Times.*

'The disreputable lingo of Cockayne is henceforth justified before the world; for a man of genius has taken it in hand, and has shown, beyond all cavilling, that in its way it also is a medium for literature. You are grateful, and you say to yourself, half in envy and half in admiration: "Here is a *book*; here, or one is a Dutchman, is one of the books of the year."'—*National Observer.*

'"Barrack-Room Ballads" contains some of the best work that Mr. Kipling has ever done, which is saying a good deal. "Fuzzy-Wuzzy," "Gunga Din," and "Tommy," are, in our opinion, altogether superior to anything of the kind that English literature has hitherto produced.'—*Athenæum.*

'These ballads are as wonderful in their descriptive power as they are vigorous in their dramatic force. There are few ballads in the English language more stirring than "The Ballad of East and West," worthy to stand by the Border ballads of Scott.'—*Spectator.*

'The ballads teem with imagination, they palpitate with emotion. We read them with laughter and tears; the metres throb in our pulses, the cunningly ordered words tingle with life; and if this be not poetry, what is?'—*Pall Mall Gazette.*

Henley. LYRA HEROICA: An Anthology selected from the best English Verse of the 16th, 17th, 18th, and 19th Centuries. By WILLIAM ERNEST HENLEY, Author of 'A Book of Verse,' 'Views and Reviews,' etc. *Crown 8vo. Stamped gilt buckram, gilt top, edges uncut.* 6s.

Mr. Henley has brought to the task of selection an instinct alike for poetry and for chivalry which seems to us quite wonderfully, and even unerringly, right.'—*Guardian.*

Tomson. A SUMMER NIGHT, AND OTHER POEMS. By GRAHAM R. TOMSON. With Frontispiece by A. TOMSON. *Fcap. 8vo.* 3s. 6d.

An edition on hand-made paper, limited to 50 copies. 10s. 6d. *net.*

'Mrs. Tomson holds perhaps the very highest rank among poetesses of English birth. This selection will help her reputation.'—*Black and White.*

Ibsen. BRAND. A Drama by HENRIK IBSEN. Translated by WILLIAM WILSON. *Crown 8vo. Second Edition.* 3s. 6d.

'The greatest world-poem of the nineteenth century next to "Faust." "Brand" will have an astonishing interest for Englishmen. It is in the same set with "Agamemnon," with "Lear," with the literature that we now instinctively regard as high and holy.'—*Daily Chronicle.*

"Q." GREEN BAYS: Verses and Parodies. By "Q.," Author of 'Dead Man's Rock' etc. *Second Edition. Fcap. 8vo.* 3s. 6d.

'The verses display a rare and versatile gift of parody, great command of metre, and a very pretty turn of humour.'—*Times.*

"A. G." VERSES TO ORDER. By "A. G." *Cr. 8vo.* 2s. 6d. *net.*

A small volume of verse by a writer whose initials are well known to Oxford men 'A capital specimen of light academic poetry. These verses are very bright and engaging, easy and sufficiently witty.'—*St. James's Gazette.*

Hosken. VERSES BY THE WAY. By J. D. HOSKEN. Printed on laid paper, and bound in buckram, gilt top. 5s. A small edition on hand-made paper. *Price* 12s. 6d. *net.*

A Volume of Lyrics and Sonnets by J. D. Hosken, the Postman Poet, of Helston, Cornwall, whose interesting career is now more or less well known to the literary public. Q, the Author of 'The Splendid Spur,' etc., writes a critical and biographical introduction.

Scott. THE MAGIC HOUSE AND OTHER VERSES. By DUNCAN C. SCOTT. *Extra Post 8vo, bound in buckram.* 5s.

Langbridge. BALLADS OF THE BRAVE: Poems of Chivalry, Enterprise, Courage, and Constancy, from the Earliest Times to the Present Day. Edited, with Notes, by Rev. F. LANGBRIDGE. *Crown 8vo. Buckram* 3s. 6d. School Edition, 2s. 6d.

'A very happy conception happily carried out. These "Ballads of the Brave" are intended to suit the real tastes of boys, and will suit the taste of the great majority. —*Spectator.* 'The book is full of splendid things.'—*World.*

General Literature

Collingwood. JOHN RUSKIN: His Life and Work. By W. G. COLLINGWOOD, M.A., late Scholar of University College, Oxford, Author of the 'Art Teaching of John Ruskin,' Editor of Mr. Ruskin's Poems. 2 *vols.* 8vo. 32s. *Second Edition.*

This important work is written by Mr. Collingwood, who has been for some years Mr. Ruskin's private secretary, and who has had unique advantages in obtaining materials for this book from Mr. Ruskin himself and from his friends. It contains a large amount of new matter, and of letters which have never been published, and is, in fact, a full and authoritative biography of Mr. Ruskin. The book contains numerous portraits of Mr. Ruskin, including a coloured one from a

water-colour portrait by himself, and also 13 sketches, never before published, by Mr. Ruskin and Mr. Arthur Severn. A bibliography is added.
'No more magnificent volumes have been published for a long time. . . .'—*Times.*
'This most lovingly written and most profoundly interesting book.'—*Daily News.*
'It is long since we have had a biography with such varied delights of substance and of form. Such a book is a pleasure for the day, and a joy for ever.'—*Daily Chronicle.*
'Mr. Ruskin could not well have been more fortunate in his biographer.'—*Globe.*
'A noble monument of a noble subject. One of the most beautiful books about one of the noblest lives of our century.'—*Glasgow Herald.*

Gladstone. THE SPEECHES AND PUBLIC ADDRESSES OF THE RT. HON. W. E. GLADSTONE, M.P. With Notes and Introductions. Edited by A. W. HUTTON, M.A. (Librarian of the Gladstone Library), and H. J. COHEN, M.A. With Portraits. 8vo. *Vol. X.* 12s. 6d.

Russell. THE LIFE OF ADMIRAL LORD COLLINGWOOD. By W. CLARK RUSSELL, Author of 'The Wreck of the Grosvenor.' With Illustrations by F. BRANGWYN. 8vo. 15s.
'A really good book.'—*Saturday Review.*
'A most excellent and wholesome book, which we should like to see in the hands of every boy in the country.'—*St. James's Gazette.*

Clark. THE COLLEGES OF OXFORD: Their History and their Traditions. By Members of the University. Edited by A. CLARK, M.A., Fellow and Tutor of Lincoln College. 8vo. 12s. 6d.
'Whether the reader approaches the book as a patriotic member of a college, as an antiquary, or as a student of the organic growth of college foundation, it will amply reward his attention.'—*Times.*
'A delightful book, learned and lively.'—*Academy.*
'A work which will certainly be appealed to for many years as the standard book on the Colleges of Oxford.'—*Athenæum.*

Wells. OXFORD AND OXFORD LIFE. By Members of the University. Edited by J. WELLS, M.A., Fellow and Tutor of Wadham College. *Crown 8vo.* 3s. 6d.
This work contains an account of life at Oxford—intellectual, social, and religious—a careful estimate of necessary expenses, a review of recent changes, a statement of the present position of the University, and chapters on Women's Education, aids to study, and University Extension.
'We congratulate Mr. Wells on the production of a readable and intelligent account of Oxford as it is at the present time, written by persons who are, with hardly an exception, possessed of a close acquaintance with the system and life of the University.'—*Athenæum.*

MESSRS. METHUEN'S LIST   11

Perrens. THE HISTORY OF FLORENCE FROM THE TIME OF THE MEDICIS TO THE FALL OF THE REPUBLIC. By F. T. PERRENS. Translated by HANNAH LYNCH. In three volumes. *Vol. I.* 8vo. 12s. 6d.

This is a translation from the French of the best history of Florence in existence. This volume covers a period of profound interest—political and literary—and is written with great vivacity.

This is a standard book by an honest and intelligent historian, who has deserved well of his countrymen, and of all who are interested in Italian history.'—*Manchester Guardian.*

Browning. GUELPHS AND GHIBELLINES: A Short History of Mediæval Italy, A.D. 1250-1409. By OSCAR BROWNING, Fellow and Tutor of King's College, Cambridge. *Second Edition.* Crown 8vo. 5s.

'A very able book.'—*Westminster Gazette.*
'A vivid picture of medæival Italy.'—*Standard.*

O'Grady. THE STORY OF IRELAND. By STANDISH O'GRADY, Author of 'Finn and his Companions.' *Cr.* 8vo. 2s. 6d.

'Novel and very fascinating history. Wonderfully alluring.'—*Cork Examiner.*
'Most delightful, most stimulating. Its racy humour, its original imaginings, its perfectly unique history, make it one of the freshest, breeziest volumes.'—*Methodist Times.*
'A survey at once graphic, acute, and quaintly written.'—*Times.*

Dixon. ENGLISH POETRY FROM BLAKE TO BROWNING. By W. M. DIXON, M.A. *Crown 8vo.* 3s. 6d.

A Popular Account of the Poetry of the Century.
'Scholarly in conception, and full of sound and suggestive criticism.'—*Times.*
'The book is remarkable for freshness of thought expressed in graceful language.'—*Manchester Examiner.*

Bowden. THE EXAMPLE OF BUDDHA: Being Quotations from Buddhist Literature for each Day in the Year. Compiled by E. M. BOWDEN. With Preface by Sir EDWIN ARNOLD. *Third Edition.* 16mo. 2s. 6d.

Ditchfield. OUR ENGLISH VILLAGES: Their Story and their Antiquities. By P. H. DITCHFIELD, M.A., F.R.H.S., Rector of Barkham, Berks. *Post 8vo.* 2s. 6d. Illustrated.

'An extremely amusing and interesting little book, which should find a place in every parochial library.'—*Guardian.*

Ditchfield. OLD ENGLISH SPORTS. By P. H. DITCH-
FIELD, M.A. *Crown 8vo.* 2s. 6d. Illustrated.
'A charming account of old English Sports.'—*Morning Post.*

Massee. A MONOGRAPH OF THE MYXOGASTRES. By
GEORGE MASSEE. With 12 Coloured Plates. *Royal 8vo.* 18s. *net.*
'A work much in advance of any book in the language treating of this group of organisms. It is indispensable to every student of the Mxyogastres. The coloured plates deserve high praise for their accuracy and execution.'—*Nature.*

Bushill. PROFIT SHARING AND THE LABOUR QUESTION. By T. W. BUSHILL, a Profit Sharing Employer. With an Introduction by SEDLEY TAYLOR, Author of 'Profit Sharing between Capital and Labour.' *Crown 8vo.* 2s. 6d.

John Beever. PRACTICAL FLY-FISHING, Founded on Nature, by JOHN BEEVER, late of the Thwaite House, Coniston. A New Edition, with a Memoir of the Author by W. G. COLLINGWOOD, M.A., Author of 'The Life and Work of John Ruskin,' etc. Also additional Notes and a chapter on Char-Fishing, by A. and A. R. SEVERN. With a specially designed title-page. *Crown 8vo.* 3s. 6d.
A little book on Fly-Fishing by an old friend of Mr. Ruskin. It has been out of print for some time, and being still much in request, is now issued with a Memoir of the Author by W. G. Collingwood.

Theology

Driver. SERMONS ON SUBJECTS CONNECTED WITH THE OLD TESTAMENT. By S. R. DRIVER, D.D., Canon of Christ Church, Regius Professor of Hebrew in the University of Oxford. *Crown 8vo.* 6s.
'A welcome companion to the author's famous 'Introduction.' No man can read these discourses without feeling that Dr. Driver is fully alive to the deeper teaching of the Old Testament.'—*Guardian.*

Cheyne. FOUNDERS OF OLD TESTAMENT CRITICISM: Biographical, Descriptive, and Critical Studies. By T. K. CHEYNE, D.D., Oriel Professor of the Interpretation of Holy Scripture at Oxford. *Large crown 8vo.* 7s. 6d.
This important book is a historical sketch of O.T. Criticism in the form of biographical studies from the days of Eichhorn to those of Driver and Robertson Smith. It is the only book of its kind in English.
'The volume is one of great interest and value. It displays all the author's well-known ability and learning, and its opportune publication has laid all students of theology, and specially of Bible criticism, under weighty obligation.'—*Scotsman.*
'A very learned and instructive work.'—*Times.*

Prior. CAMBRIDGE SERMONS. Edited by C. H. PRIOR, M.A., Fellow and Tutor of Pembroke College. *Crown 8vo. 6s.*

A volume of sermons preached before the University of Cambridge by various preachers, including the Archbishop of Canterbury and Bishop Westcott.

'A representative collection. Bishop Westcott's is a noble sermon.'—*Guardian.*
'Full of thoughtfulness and dignity.'—*Record.*

Burne. PARSON AND PEASANT: Chapters of their Natural History. By J. B. BURNE, M.A. *Cr. 8vo. 5s.*

'"Parson and Peasant" is a book not only to be interested in, but to learn something from—a book which may prove a help to many a clergyman, and broaden the hearts and ripen the charity of laymen.'—*Derby Mercury.*

Cunningham. THE PATH TOWARDS KNOWLEDGE: Essays on Questions of the Day. By W. CUNNINGHAM, D.D., Fellow of Trinity College, Cambridge, Professor of Economics at King's College, London. *Crown 8vo. 4s. 6d.*

Essays on Marriage and Population, Socialism, Money, Education, Positivism, etc.

James. CURIOSITIES OF CHRISTIAN HISTORY PRIOR TO THE REFORMATION. By CROAKE JAMES, Author of 'Curiosities of Law and Lawyers.' *Crown 8vo. 7s. 6d.*

'This volume contains a great deal of quaint and curious matter, affording some "particulars of the interesting persons, episodes, and events from the Christian's point of view during the first fourteen centuries." Wherever we dip into his pages we find something worth dipping into.'—*John Bull.*

Lock. THE LIFE OF JOHN KEBLE. By WALTER LOCK, M.A. With Portrait from a painting by GEORGE RICHMOND, R.A. *Crown 8vo. Buckram 5s. Fifth Edition.*

'A fine portrait of one of the most saintly characters of our age, and a valuable contribution to the history of that Oxford Movement.'—*Times.*

Kaufmann. CHARLES KINGSLEY. By M. KAUFMANN, M.A. *Crown 8vo. Buckram. 5s.*

A biography of Kingsley, especially dealing with his achievements in social reform.
'The author has certainly gone about his work with conscientiousness and industry.'—*Sheffield Daily Telegraph.*

Oliphant. THOMAS CHALMERS: A Biography. By Mrs. OLIPHANT. With Portrait. *Crown 8vo. Buckram, 5s.*

'A well-executed biography, worthy of its author and of the remarkable man who is its subject. Mrs. Oliphant relates lucidly and dramatically the important part which Chalmers played in the memorable secession.'—*Times.*

MESSRS. METHUEN'S LIST

Leaders of Religion

Edited by H. C. BEECHING, M.A. *With Portrait, crown 8vo.* 2s. 6d.

A series of short biographies of the most prominent leaders of religious life and thought.

2/6

The following are ready—

CARDINAL NEWMAN. By R. H. HUTTON.

'Few who read this book will fail to be struck by the wonderful insight it displays into the nature of the Cardinal's genius and the spirit of his life.'—WILFRID WARD, in the *Tablet*.

'Full of knowledge, excellent in method, and intelligent in criticism. We regard it as wholly admirable.'—*Academy*.

JOHN WESLEY. By J. H. OVERTON, M.A.

'It is well done: the story is clearly told, proportion is duly observed, and there is no lack either of discrimination or of sympathy.'—*Manchester Guardian*.

BISHOP WILBERFORCE. By G. W. DANIEL, M.A.

CHARLES SIMEON. By H. C. G. MOULE, M.A.

CARDINAL MANNING. By A. W. HUTTON, M.A.

Other volumes will be announced in due course.

WORKS BY S. BARING GOULD.

OLD COUNTRY LIFE. With Sixty-seven Illustrations by W. PARKINSON, F. D. BEDFORD, and F. MASEY. *Large Crown 8vo, cloth super extra, top edge gilt,* 10s. 6d. *Fourth and Cheaper Edition.* 6s.

'"Old Country Life," as healthy wholesome reading, full of breezy life and movement, full of quaint stories vigorously told, will not be excelled by any book to be published throughout the year. Sound, hearty, and English to the core.'—*World*.

HISTORIC ODDITIES AND STRANGE EVENTS. *Third Edition. Crown 8vo.* 6s.

'A collection of exciting and entertaining chapters. The whole volume is delightful reading.'—*Times*.

FREAKS OF FANATICISM. *Third Edition. Crown 8vo.* 6s.

'Mr. Baring Gould has a keen eye for colour and effect, and the subjects he has chosen give ample scope to his descriptive and analytic faculties. A perfectly fascinating book.'—*Scottish Leader*.

SONGS OF THE WEST: Traditional Ballads and Songs of the West of England, with their Traditional Melodies. Collected by S. BARING GOULD, M.A., and H. FLEETWOOD SHEPPARD, M.A. Arranged for Voice and Piano. In 4 Parts (containing 25 Songs each), *Parts I., II., III.*, 3s. each. *Part IV.*, 5s. *In one Vol., roan*, 15s.

'A rich and varied collection of humour, pathos, grace, and poetic fancy.'—*Saturday Review.*

YORKSHIRE ODDITIES AND STRANGE EVENTS.
Fourth Edition. Crown 8vo. 6s.

STRANGE SURVIVALS AND SUPERSTITIONS.
With Illustrations. By S. BARING GOULD. *Crown 8vo. Second Edition. 6s.*

A book on such subjects as Foundations, Gables, Holes, Gallows, Raising the Hat, Old Ballads, etc. etc. It traces in a most interesting manner their origin and history.

'We have read Mr. Baring Gould's book from beginning to end. It is full of quaint and various information, and there is not a dull page in it.'—*Notes and Queries.*

THE TRAGEDY OF THE CAESARS:
The Emperors of the Julian and Claudian Lines. With numerous Illustrations from Busts, Gems, Cameos, etc. By S. BARING GOULD, Author of 'Mehalah,' etc. *Second Edition.* 2 vols. *Royal 8vo.* 30s.

'A most splendid and fascinating book on a subject of undying interest. The great feature of the book is the use the author has made of the existing portraits of the Caesars, and the admirable critical subtlety he has exhibited in dealing with this line of research. It is brilliantly written, and the illustrations are supplied on a scale of profuse magnificence.'—*Daily Chronicle.*

'The volumes will in no sense disappoint the general reader. Indeed, in their way, there is nothing in any sense so good in English. . . . Mr. Baring Gould has presented his narrative in such a way as not to make one dull page.'—*Athenæum.*

MR. BARING GOULD'S NOVELS.

'To say that a book is by the author of "Mehalah" is to imply that it contains a story cast on strong lines, containing dramatic possibilities, vivid and sympathetic descriptions of Nature, and a wealth of ingenious imagery.'—*Speaker.*

'That whatever Mr. Baring Gould writes is well worth reading, is a conclusion that may be very generally accepted. His views of life are fresh and vigorous, his language pointed and characteristic, the incidents of which he makes use are striking and original, his characters are life-like, and though somewhat exceptional people, are drawn and coloured with artistic force. Add to this that his descriptions of scenes and scenery are painted with the loving eyes and skilled hands of a master of his art, that he is always fresh and never dull, and under such conditions it is no wonder that readers have gained confidence both in his power of amusing and satisfying them, and that year by year his popularity widens.'—*Court Circular.*

IN THE ROAR OF THE SEA: A Tale of the Cornish Coast. *New Edition.* 6s.

MRS. CURGENVEN OF CURGENVEN. *Third Edition.* 6s.
A powerful and characteristic story of Devon life. The 'Graphic' speaks of it as *a novel of vigorous humour and sustained power*; the 'Sussex Daily News' says that *the swing of the narrative is splendid*; and the 'Speaker' mentions its *bright imaginative power.*

CHEAP JACK ZITA. By S. BARING GOULD. *Crown 8vo.* 6s.
A Romance of the Ely Fen District in 1815.
'A powerful drama of human passion.'—*Westminster Gazette.*
'A story worthy the author.'—*National Observer.*

ARMINELL: A Social Romance. *New Edition. Crown 8vo.* 3s. 6d.

URITH: A Story of Dartmoor. *Third Edition. Crown 8vo.* 3s. 6d.
'The author is at his best.'—*Times.*
'He has nearly reached the high water-mark of "Mehalah."'—*National Observer.*

MARGERY OF QUETHER, and other Stories. *Crown 8vo.* 3s. 6d.

JACQUETTA, and other Stories. *Crown 8vo.* 3s. 6d.

Fiction

SIX SHILLING NOVELS

Corelli. BARABBAS: A DREAM OF THE WORLD'S TRAGEDY. By MARIE CORELLI, Author of 'A Romance of Two Worlds,' 'Vendetta,' etc. *Seventh Edition. Crown 8vo.* 6s.
Miss Corelli's new romance has been received with much disapprobation by the secular papers, and with warm welcome by the religious papers. By the former she has been accused of blasphemy and bad taste; 'a gory nightmare'; 'a hideous travesty'; 'grotesque vulgarisation'; 'unworthy of criticism'; 'vulgar redundancy'; 'sickening details'—these are some of the secular flowers of speech. On the other hand, the 'Guardian' praises 'the dignity of its conceptions, the reserve round the Central Figure, the fine imagery of the scene and circumstance, so much that is elevating and devout'; the 'Illustrated Church News' styles the book 'reverent and artistic, broad based on the rock of our common nature, and appealing to what is best in it'; the 'Christian World' says it is written 'by one who has more than conventional reverence, who has tried to tell the story that it may be read again with open and attentive eyes'; the 'Church of England Pulpit' welcomes 'a book which teems with faith without any appearance of irreverence.'

MESSRS. METHUEN'S LIST

Benson. DODO: A DETAIL OF THE DAY. By E. F.
BENSON. *Crown 8vo. Thirteenth Edition.* 6s.

A story of society by a new writer, full of interest and power, which has attracted by its brilliance universal attention. The best critics were cordial in their praise. The 'Guardian' spoke of 'Dody' as *unusually clever and interesting*; the 'Spectator' called it *a delightfully witty sketch of society*; the 'Speaker' said the dialogue was *a perpetual feast of epigram and paradox*; the 'Athenæum' spoke of the author as *a writer of quite exceptional ability*; the 'Academy' praised his *amazing cleverness*; the 'World' said the book was *brilliantly written*; and half-a-dozen papers declared there was *not a dull page in the book*.

Norris. HIS GRACE. By W. E. NORRIS, Author of 'Mademoiselle de Mersac.' *Third Edition. Crown 8vo.* 6s.

An edition in one volume of a novel which in its two volume form quickly ran through two editions.

'The characters are delineated by the author with his characteristic skill and vivacity, and the story is told with that ease of manners and Thackerayean insight which give strength of flavour to Mr. Norris's novels No one can depict the Englishwoman of the better classes with more subtlety.'—*Glasgow Herald.*

'Mr. Norris has drawn a really fine character in the Duke of Hurstbourne, at once unconventional and very true to the conventionalities of life, weak and strong in a breath, capable of inane follies and heroic decisions, yet not so definitely portrayed as to relieve a reader of the necessity of study on his own behalf.'—*Athenæum.*

Parker. MRS. FALCHION. By GILBERT PARKER, Author of 'Pierre and His People.' *New Edition in one volume.* 6s.

Mr. Parker's second book has received a warm welcome. The 'Athenæum' called it *a splendid study of character*; the 'Pall Mall Gazette' spoke of the writing as *but little behind anything that has been done by any writer of our time*; the 'St. James'' called it *a very striking and admirable novel*; and the 'Westminster Gazette' applied to it the epithet of *distinguished.*

Parker. PIERRE AND HIS PEOPLE. By GILBERT PARKER. *Crown 8vo. Buckram.* 6s.

'Stories happily conceived and finely executed. There is strength and genius in Mr. Parker's style.'—*Daily Telegraph.*

Anthony Hope. A CHANGE OF AIR: A Novel. By ANTHONY HOPE, Author of 'Mr. Witt's Widow,' etc. 1 *vol. Crown 8vo.* 6s.

A bright story by Mr. Hope, who has, the *Athenæum* says, 'a decided outlook and individuality of his own.'

'A graceful, vivacious comedy, true to human nature. The characters are traced with a masterly hand.'—*Times.*

Pryce. TIME AND THE WOMAN. By RICHARD PRYCE, Author of 'Miss Maxwell's Affections,' 'The Quiet Mrs. Fleming,' etc. New and Cheaper Edition. *Crown 8vo.* 6s.

'Mr. Pryce's work recalls the style of Octave Feuillet, by its clearness, conciseness, its literary reserve.'—*Athenæum.*

Gray. ELSA. A Novel. By E. M'QUEEN GRAY. *Crown 8vo.* 6s.

'A charming novel. The characters are not only powerful sketches, but minutely and carefully finished portraits.'—*Guardian.*

Marriott Watson. DIOGENES OF LONDON and other Sketches. By H. B. MARRIOTT WATSON, Author of 'The Web of the Spider.' *Crown 8vo. Buckram.* 6s.

'By all those who delight in the uses of words, who rate the exercise of prose above the exercise of verse, who rejoice in all proofs of its delicacy and its strength, who believe that English prose is chief among the moulds of thought, by these Mr. Marriott Watson's book will be welcomed.'—*National Observer.*

Gilchrist. THE STONE DRAGON. By MURRAY GILCHRIST. *Crown 8vo. Buckram.* 6s.

A volume of stories of power so weird and original as to ensure them a ready welcome.
'The author's faults are atoned for by certain positive and admirable merits. The romances have not their counterpart in modern literature, and to read them is a unique experience.'—*National Observer.*

THREE-AND-SIXPENNY NOVELS

Norris. A DEPLORABLE AFFAIR. By W. E. NORRIS, Author of 'His Grace.' *Crown 8vo.* 3s. 6d.

'What with its interesting story, its graceful manner, and its perpetual good humour, the book is as enjoyable as any that has come from its author's pen.'—*Scotsman.*

Pearce. JACO TRELOAR. By J. H. PEARCE, Author of 'Esther Pentreath.' *New Edition. Crown 8vo.* 3s. 6d.

A tragic story of Cornish life by a writer of remarkable power, whose first novel has been highly praised by Mr. Gladstone.
The 'Spectator' speaks of Mr. Pearce as *a writer of exceptional power*; the 'Daily Telegraph' calls it *powerful and picturesque*; the 'Birmingham Post' asserts that it is *a novel of high quality.*

Esmé Stuart. A WOMAN OF FORTY. By ESMÉ STUART, Author of 'Muriel's Marriage,' 'Virginie's Husband,' etc. *New Edition. Crown 8vo. 3s. 6d.*

'The story is well written, and some of the scenes show great dramatic power.'—*Daily Chronicle.*

Fenn. THE STAR GAZERS. By G. MANVILLE FENN, Author of 'Eli's Children,' etc. *New Edition. Cr. 8vo. 3s. 6d.*

'A stirring romance.'—*Western Morning News.*

'Told with all the dramatic power for which Mr. Fenn is conspicuous.'—*Bradford Observer.*

Dickinson. A VICAR'S WIFE. By EVELYN DICKINSON. *Crown 8vo. 3s. 6d.*

Prowse. THE POISON OF ASPS. By R. ORTON PROWSE. *Crown 8vo. 3s. 6d.*

Lynn Linton. THE TRUE HISTORY OF JOSHUA DAVIDSON, Christian and Communist. By E. LYNN LINTON. Eleventh Edition. *Post 8vo.* 1s.

Methuen's Novel Series

A series of copyright Novels, by well-known Authors, bound in red buckram, at the price of three shillings and sixpence. The first volumes are:— **3/6**

1. JACQUETTA. By S. BARING GOULD, Author of 'Mehalah,' etc.
2. ARMINELL: A Social Romance. By S. BARING GOULD Author of 'Mehalah,' etc.
3. MARGERY OF QUETHER. By S. BARING GOULD.
4. URITH. By S. BARING GOULD.
5. DERRICK VAUGHAN, NOVELIST. With Portrait of Author. By EDNA LYALL, Author of 'Donovan,' etc.
6. JACK'S FATHER. By W. E. NORRIS.

   Other Volumes will be announced in due course.

HALF-CROWN NOVELS

A Series of Novels by popular Authors, tastefully bound in cloth.

2/6

1. THE PLAN OF CAMPAIGN. By F. MABEL ROBINSON.
2. DISENCHANTMENT. By F. MABEL ROBINSON.
3. MR. BUTLER'S WARD. By F. MABEL ROBINSON.
4. HOVENDEN, V.C. By F. MABEL ROBINSON.
5. ELI'S CHILDREN. By G. MANVILLE FENN.
6. A DOUBLE KNOT. By G. MANVILLE FENN.
7. DISARMED. By M. BETHAM EDWARDS.
8. A LOST ILLUSION. By LESLIE KEITH.
9. A MARRIAGE AT SEA. By W. CLARK RUSSELL.
10. IN TENT AND BUNGALOW. By the Author of 'Indian Idylls.'
11. MY STEWARDSHIP. By E. M'QUEEN GRAY.
12. A REVEREND GENTLEMAN. By J. M. COBBAN.
13. THE STORY OF CHRIS. By ROWLAND GREY.

Other volumes will be announced in due course.

Books for Boys and Girls

Baring Gould. THE ICELANDER'S SWORD. By S. BARING GOULD, Author of 'Mehalah,' etc. With Twenty-nine Illustrations by J. MOYR SMITH. *Crown 8vo. 6s.*

A stirring story of Iceland, written for boys by the author of 'In the Roar of the Sea.'

Cuthell. TWO LITTLE CHILDREN AND CHING. By EDITH E. CUTHELL. Profusely Illustrated. *Crown 8vo. Cloth, gilt edges. 6s.*

Another story, with a dog hero, by the author of the very popular 'Only a Guard-Room Dog.'

Blake. TODDLEBEN'S HERO. By M. M. BLAKE, Author of 'The Siege of Norwich Castle.' With 36 Illustrations. *Crown 8vo. 5s.*

A story of military life for children.

Cuthell. ONLY A GUARD-ROOM DOG. By Mrs. CUTHELL. With 16 Illustrations by W. PARKINSON. *Square Crown 8vo.* 6s.

'This is a charming story. Tangle was but a little mongrel Skye terrier, but he had a big heart in his little body, and played a hero's part more than once. The book can be warmly recommended.'—*Standard.*

Collingwood. THE DOCTOR OF THE JULIET. By HARRY COLLINGWOOD, Author of 'The Pirate Island,' etc. Illustrated by GORDON BROWNE. *Crown 8vo.* 6s.

'"The Doctor of the Juliet," well illustrated by Gordon Browne, is one of Harry Collingwood's best efforts.'—*Morning Post.*

Clark Russell. MASTER ROCKAFELLAR'S VOYAGE. By W. CLARK RUSSELL, Author of 'The Wreck of the Grosvenor,' etc. Illustrated by GORDON BROWNE. *Crown 8vo.* 3s. 6d.

'Mr. Clark Russell's story of "Master Rockafellar's Voyage" will be among the favourites of the Christmas books. There is a rattle and "go" all through it, and its illustrations are charming in themselves, and very much above the average in the way in which they are produced.'—*Guardian.*

Manville Fenn. SYD BELTON : Or, The Boy who would not go to Sea. By G. MANVILLE FENN, Author of 'In the King's Name,' etc. Illustrated by GORDON BROWNE. *Crown 8vo.* 3s. 6d.

'Who among the young story-reading public will not rejoice at the sight of the old combination, so often proved admirable—a story by Manville Fenn, illustrated by Gordon Browne? The story, too, is one of the good old sort, full of life and vigour, breeziness and fun.'—*Journal of Education.*

The Peacock Library

A Series of Books for Girls by well-known Authors, handsomely bound in blue and silver, and well illustrated. Crown 8vo. **3/6**

1. A PINCH OF EXPERIENCE. By L. B. WALFORD.
2. THE RED GRANGE. By Mrs. MOLESWORTH.
3. THE SECRET OF MADAME DE MONLUC. By the Author of 'Mdle Mori.'
4. DUMPS. By Mrs. PARR, Author of 'Adam and Eve.'
5. OUT OF THE FASHION. By L. T. MEADE.
6. A GIRL OF THE PEOPLE. By L. T. MEADE.
7. HEPSY GIPSY. By L. T. MEADE.
8. THE HONOURABLE MISS. By L. T. MEADE.
9. MY LAND OF BEULAH. By Mrs. LEITH ADAMS.

MUTUAL THRIFT. By Rev. J. FROME WILKINSON, M.A., Author of 'The Friendly Society Movement.'

PROBLEMS OF POVERTY : An Inquiry into the Industrial Conditions of the Poor. By J. A. HOBSON, M.A.

THE COMMERCE OF NATIONS. By C. F. BASTABLE, M.A., Professor of Economics at Trinity College, Dublin.

THE ALIEN INVASION. By W. H. WILKINS, B.A., Secretary to the Society for Preventing the Immigration of Destitute Aliens.

THE RURAL EXODUS. By P. ANDERSON GRAHAM.

LAND NATIONALIZATION. By HAROLD COX, B.A.

A SHORTER WORKING DAY. By H. DE B. GIBBINS and R. A. HADFIELD, of the Hecla Works, Sheffield.

BACK TO THE LAND: An Inquiry into the Cure for Rural Depopulation. By H. E. MOORE.

Methuen's Commercial Series

BRITISH COMMERCE AND COLONIES FROM ELIZABETH TO VICTORIA. By H. DE B. GIBBINS, M.A., Author of 'The Industrial History of England,' etc., etc. 2s.

A MANUAL OF FRENCH COMMERCIAL CORRESPONDENCE. By S. E. BALLY, Modern Language Master at the Manchester Grammar School. 2s.

COMMERCIAL GEOGRAPHY, with special reference to Trade Routes, New Markets, and Manufacturing Districts. By L. D. LYDE, M.A., of The Academy, Glasgow. 2s.

COMMERCIAL EXAMINATION PAPERS. By H. DE B. GIBBINS, M.A. 1s. 6d.

THE ECONOMICS OF COMMERCE. By H. DE B. GIBBINS, M.A. 1s. 6d.

Edinburgh: T. and A. CONSTABLE, Printers to Her Majesty.

www.ingramcontent.com/pod-product-compliance
Lightning Source LLC
Chambersburg PA
CBHW020905230426
43666CB00008B/1323